THE LITERATURE OF DEATH AND DYING

DEATH, GRIEF, AND MOURNING

Geoffrey Gorer

ARNO PRESS

A New York Times Company

New York / 1977

Reprint Edition 1977 by Arno Press Inc.

Copyright © 1965 by Geoffrey Gorer

Reprinted by arrangement with
  Doubleday & Company, Inc.

THE LITERATURE OF DEATH AND DYING
ISBN for complete set: 0-405-09550-3
See last pages of this volume for titles.

Manufactured in the United States of America

———◆———

Library of Congress Cataloging in Publication Data
Gorer, Geoffrey, 1905-
    Death, grief, and mourning.

    (The Literature of death and dying)
    First published in London under title: Death, grief,
and mourning in contemporary Britain.
    Reprint of the ed. published by Doubleday, Garden City,
N. Y.
    Bibliography: p.
    1. Funeral rites and ceremonies--Great Britain.
2. Mourning customs--Great Britain. 3. Bereavement.
I. Title. II. Series.
[GT3243.G6 1977]   393'.9'0941   76-19573
ISBN 0-405-09571-6

DEATH, GRIEF, AND
MOURNING

DEATH, GRIEF, AND MOURNING

Geoffrey Gorer

DOUBLEDAY & COMPANY, INC.
GARDEN CITY, NEW YORK
1965

Lines from "Sweeney Agonistes" by T. S. Eliot are reprinted by
permission of Harcourt, Brace & World, Inc.

Library of Congress Catalog Card Number 65–19875
Copyright © 1965 by Geoffrey Gorer
All Rights Reserved
Printed in the United States of America
First Edition in the United States of America

CONTENTS

FOREWORD

The research on which this book is based was made possible by grants from the *Sunday Times* and the Cresset Press. The survey was carried out by Research Services Ltd. and the tables prepared by them. The longer interviews were carried out by myself with the assistance of Mr. David Tomlinson. The survey interviews were made in April and May 1963, the longer interviews in October and November.

I was fortunate in getting very willing collaboration from many of the people I talked with. In order to safeguard their anonymity as completely as possible, I have departed from the customary pattern of books of this kind, in that I am only stating the region in which the informants were interviewed and, where it seems relevant, an indication of their occupation. I have given all informants who are quoted more than once an arbitrary number; an index of these numbers will make it possible to trace the experience and views of any informant on the topics discussed in the different chapters.

In Appendix Two I reproduce the questionnaire which was used by Research Services Ltd. and some of the relevant tables. I also list all the areas in which interviews were conducted.

I should like to express my gratitude to all the people and institutions listed above who have assisted me in this work; my deepest thanks are due to those mourners who spoke to me so frankly in the trust that by disclosing their own sufferings they might help to alleviate those of others.

In my recent books, such as *The American People, The*

People of Great Russia and *Exploring English Character*,
I attempted to identify the psychological components of
behaviour and institutions which had customarily been
treated as sociological, cultural or political. In this study
I am attempting to identify the sociological and cultural
implications of a situation—bereavement—which is customarily treated as exclusively or predominantly private
and psychological. Since societies are composed of human
beings, I believe that all social behaviour has a psychological component which can be isolated and described; since
all human beings are members of a society, I believe that
their emotional responses have sociological or anthropo-
logical implications which can be isolated and described.
Although the treatment of the data in this book is different from that in the earlier studies, I feel in this case
that this is a more appropriate technique for analysing this
aspect of man-in-society.

May, 1964   G. G.

INTRODUCTION TO THE
AMERICAN EDITION

The data and illustrations in this book—I cannot deny it
—are exclusively British; but the main theme of the book,
the social denial and the individual repudiation of mourning, is, I believe, as apposite to the majority of the inhabitants of the United States as it is to the majority of the
inhabitants of the United Kingdom. Certainly in the
areas of the U.S.A. with which I am most familiar the
wearing of mourning and the formal withdrawal from social life for a period after the occurrence of death is as
uncommon as it is in most of Britain.

It is interesting to speculate why this should be so, for
the causes which I have suggested were operative in Britain do not seem as if they could have had a similar impact
in the U.S.A. The involvement of the United States in
the First World War was very much briefer than was that
of Britain, and the casualties, in proportion to the population, were relatively few; it does not seem likely that
this war could have had a directly traumatic effect on the
whole population of America as it undoubtedly did in
Britain. If one can take regular attendance at church services as an index of religious feeling, the decline in religious belief, which I have now twice documented for England, has no parallel in most of the United States.

It seems to me possible that one reason for the dis-
avowal of mourning in the United States over the last
forty years may have been the increasing pressure of what
Leites and Wolfenstein called "fun-morality," the ethical
duty to enjoy oneself (to prove that one is psychologically

well-adjusted) and the generous imperative to do nothing
which might diminish the enjoyment of others, so that
the right to the pursuit of happiness has been turned into
an obligation. Public and even private mourning may be
felt as contravening this ethic.

I suppose the most striking contrast between the British and the American handling of death lies in the treatment of the body between death and disposal, and in the
expense involved in the funeral or cremation, topics on
which Mesdames Mitford and Harmer have lavished their
wit and indignation. I found no analogue in Britain to the
beautifying and rejuvenating of the corpse, and embalming still seems to be a very uncommon practice (the difference in climate may be in part responsible); and any
form of religious ritual performed with the body of the
dead person visible (in contrast to the closed coffin) seems
to be confined exclusively to Roman Catholic wakes, when
the Rosary may be recited. All my Roman Catholic informants were poor people, which may account for the
fact that they made so little mention of cards saying that
masses were being said for the soul of the person
mourned; I have reason to believe that this is often a
source of comfort to more prosperous Roman Catholic
mourners.

Because England has an established church which ac-
cords burial rights to all parishioners at a very moderate
fee, the expense and display of a funeral were always a
matter of individual choice. The very simple and cheap
funeral was always available; but it was rejected, as a
disgrace, by most of the population until well into the
present century. Dickens documents, with Betty Higden
in *Our Mutual Friend*, the horror felt by the poor at the
possibility of being buried "by the parish"; and in *Martin*

Chuzzlewit and *David Copperfield* he describes the elaborate funerals then current in all classes of society. A great majority of the working population paid a few pence weekly out of their exiguous wages into an insurance policy which would provide the money for an elaborate funeral; this was, apparently, one of the most profitable lines in insurance business.

The rejection of lavish funeral display in Britain seems to have started among the intellectual professional classes in the first decade of this century. In their earnest rationalism they stigmatized the then current funeral practices as "barbarous" and economically wasteful; it is hard to tell now whether they were more appalled at the "superstition" or the "extravagance." They did, however, provide a model for simple and economical funerals which was available during and after the holocaust of World War One, and which was gradually acceptable to the rest of the population. As far as my evidence goes, funereal ostentation is now very uncommon indeed in Britain, though among the groups on the edge of legality the floral tributes are expensive and peculiar, perhaps a faint echo of the Chicago gangster funerals of the thirties. It is curious to note that the contemporary rejection of lavish funeral display in the United States derives from very much the same social class as in Britain half a century ago.

The fact that England and Scotland have established churches (corresponding to the Episcopalian and Presbyterian) to which all the inhabitants of these countries are presumed to belong, unless they or their parents choose differently, may in part account for the very low intensity or absence of religious belief among the majority of the British. The concept of "attending the Church of one's choice" seems to be almost entirely absent from British life. The Church of England permits a wide gamut of ritual within its services; those with the greatest amount of ritual are considered "High Church" or "Anglo-Catholic" or (partly as an in-joke) "spiky"; those with the simplest ritual are "Low Church"; and, within the larger towns, the small minority who are regular in their attendance at Church services may seek out one whose level of ritual is in accordance with their existing preferences. There are occasional conversions, typically from Anglicanism to Roman Catholicism, or from Judaism to Anglicanism; but the notion of attending services of different Nonconformist churches to discover which is personally the most satisfying is, I think, quite alien to British custom.

Compared to the United States, a very small proportion of the British population falls into ethnic groups with ties of either language or ritual to their countries of origin; post-World-War-Two immigrants from the Commonwealth apart, the only sizable groups are the Roman Catholic working class from Ireland, and the Orthodox Jews from central Europe. I think it is significant that members of these groups have relatively elaborate mourning rituals; and the large number of members of ethnic groups in the United States may well be one reason for the maintenance of elaborate funeral ceremonies. For people who feel themselves to be members of minorities these ritual gatherings may well provide evidence of group solidarity, for which members of the majority feel no conscious need; and such gatherings may be a major source of comfort and support in the first days of shock after a bereavement.

There is one factor which is relatively unimportant in Britain which may have conduced to the denial of mourning in the United States; this is the possibility of divorce.

Although divorces are by no means unknown in Britain, they are not, I think, envisaged as a probability outside the small group of café society and the entertainment professions; most British people act on the assumption that a spouse or parent will go out of one's life only through death. This is of course factually true of most American marriages and families also; but the possibility of divorce is, I think, much more in the fore-front of attention. There can be relatively few schools where there are no children of divorced parents, relatively few urban or suburban communities which do not include a divorced man or woman. This situation may well provide a basis for fantasy about the disappearance of parent or spouse, as it were a playing with the idea of loss. Since such fantasies are inadmissable while the family is still intact they must be denied expression; and when a family is in fact broken by death this denial may still be operative.

Despite the marked differences between the United States and Britain in many of their attitudes and institutions, all the evidence I possess suggests to me that there are very many parallels in the behaviour and treatment of the bereaved once the body is disposed of. In both countries private mourning is generally denied, though there is still admission of public mourning on the death of a famous figure, such as President Kennedy or Sir Winston Churchill; and the majority of both countries tend to treat mourning as morbid self-indulgence, and to give social admiration to the bereaved who hide their grief so fully that no one would guess anything had happened. It seems to me probable that the maladaptive and neurotic behaviour which I discern in Britain as a consequence of a denial of mourning has its counterparts in the United States; and I therefore presume to hope that, although all the data on which this study is founded is British, it will be found to have relevance for Americans also.

January, 1965   G. G.

AUTOBIOGRAPHICAL INTRODUCTION

Some of the most vivid memories of my early childhood are concerned with the death of Edward the Seventh. I had just turned five in May, 1910. On the Sunday morning after his death, our nanny took my brother Peter (two years my junior) and me for our customary walk on Hampstead Heath. It was a fine morning and the Heath was crowded. As we came out of Heath Street to the White Stone Pond we could see a mass of people out to enjoy the sun; and practically every woman was dressed in full mourning, in black from top to toe. Nearly all the men were in dark suits too, but that was customary for 'Sunday best'. This mass of black-garbed humanity struck me as a most depressing sight.

We used to have Sunday lunch with our parents; and there was Mother, too, dressed in black. I grizzled and nagged at Mother to get out of those horrid clothes, and finally she agreed to wear 'half-mourning'—grey or purple —in the house; but, she explained to me, she *had* to wear black when she went out. King Edward was a good king, we were very sorry that he had gone, and wearing black was a sign that we respected and missed him and shared the grief of his family. I think this made some sense to me, for I think that I knew then that Queen Mary— Princess May—was a client of my father, and so it was right that Mother should do what pleased her. But I didn't understand why everybody else had to too.

This is my first clear recollection of death and mourning. There were no deaths in my family of which I was conscious during my childhood (my mother's brother,

Alfred, had died of leukemia when I was two, and my
paternal grandmother at about the same time, but I have
no recollection of either); but I was certainly conscious
of the fact of death. The parade of funerals—horse-drawn,
of course, with black plumes and all the trimmings—was
a constant feature of street life; and we children had to
keep an eye out for them and take off our hats or caps
for the whole time that the funeral procession passed us;
it was very *rude* not to, and showed a lack of respect for
people in their great trouble. And when people were
dressed in mourning—they might be visitors or servants
or shop-assistants—we had to be quiet, and not fidget or
make a noise. As small children we learned that mourners
were in a special situation or state of mind and had to be
treated differently from others, with more consideration
and more respect; and I think our education on this
subject was typical of that period.

I have no memory of being puzzled about death; it was
something which happened to all people and to animals
too. Our dear bulldog, Billy, was smothered on one of the
spring transfers from town to country; I remember being
unhappy and angry at his unnecessary death; but not surprised. This must have taken place when I was 7 or 8,
since at 9 I went to boarding school and no longer took
part in these transfers. A family anecdote recounts that I
was found in tears on my tenth birthday, and when asked
why I was crying, explained that I had got into two figures, and so few people got into three! On some level I
had accepted the fact that I was mortal, and so were all
those I loved; but the only death that I contemplated was
natural death. Violent death was exotic, a thing which
happened in books—I was an avid reader of Conan Doyle
and, particularly, of Rider Haggard—and did not represent any sort of domestic threat.

My father was drowned in the *Lusitania* on his return from a business trip to the United States in May, 1915. As we learned later, he died heroically, giving up both his seat in one of the lifeboats and his life-belt to two women passengers, both of whom survived and visited my mother. His death was completely unforeseen, for at that period only soldiers in the firing line and Belgians were thought to be in any danger.

I learnt of the sinking of the *Lusitania* at breakfast at school. We sat at long tables, I near the bottom end, one of the masters at the head; the master would read out the war news from his newspaper, and the headline would be passed down the table. I can well remember the almost physical shock with which I heard the news, a short period during which every sound seemed to have gone out of the world; then I burst into uncontrolled sobbing and it was, it seemed, quite a time before I could explain to anybody what I was crying about. When I could be understood, I was treated with great kindness, but like an invalid; no demands were made on me, I was indulged, conversation was hushed in my presence. I cannot remember anyone, master or boy, talking seriously to me about death in general or the death of my father in particular; nor can I remember any of them making a joke in my presence.

Of course, my father's death was not confirmed immediately. There were days of agonized waiting, as survivors were picked up and brought to land, chiefly to Irish ports; even now I can barely reconstruct the agony my mother must have gone through as she waited outside the Cunard office. I think I must have been in a sort of daze during that period; my chief recollection is of being taken for brisk walks by the head master's kind sister Miss Russell, during the hours of lessons. It was the second week of May (the *Lusitania* was sunk on May 7th), and I remember very vividly that great orange oriental poppies and purple blue flag iris were flowering on the edge of the school drive; in an attempt to convey the desolation I was feeling I said to Miss Russell that I did not think I should ever be able to enjoy flowers again; at which she reprimanded me, telling me not to be morbid.

I do not remember how soon I was given black ties and had bands of crêpe sewn on to the sleeves of my suits; but I remember the first days I wore these insignia of woe feeling, despite my unhappiness, somehow distinguished, in nearly every sense of the word. I was set apart; and this was somehow fitting and comforting.

As rational hope diminished, I constructed elaborate fantasies that my father was surviving on some desert island in the Atlantic; for at least some months I put off the acceptance of his final disappearance by these dreams. I do not recall that at any time in my life I had any conviction of personal survival; it was only by such magical thinking that my father could be kept from extinction.

While he was alive, my attitude towards my father had been quite consciously ambivalent; I loved him, but I was afraid of him. This fear was mostly irrational, for I do not think he ever punished me or hurt me intentionally; he was so big, so strong, so boisterous. But there were two occasions when he was associated with fear and pain, both I think in my seventh year, at the height of the oedipal conflict. Once, when I was in bed with some sort of indigestion pain, he tickled me and made me laugh, which temporarily turned the pain into agony; insensitively he continued with this for some minutes, and I found this very hard to forgive. The same summer he took me, as was a frequent practice, sculling before breakfast up a Thames backwater near our house where we spent the summers; inadvertently he went too near a nesting swan, and we were chased by the male, its enormous wings outspread and skimming over the water, all the way back to the main stream and our house. My father was rationally frightened, for a stroke of that mighty wing could have broken a man's arm and probably killed a child; but he communicated to me quite irrational fear, panic; and thereafter he was never quite free from that association in my eyes.

Nevertheless, I most passionately wanted him not to be dead. This was not only, not even perhaps mainly, due to the sense of loss, of incompleteness; it was also apprehension of the burden of responsibility which, I felt, his death would put on me. As an eldest son I had learned that I was my father's representative in his absence; I don't know whence I derived this belief, but it must have been common enough in Edwardian nurseries, for E. Nesbit puts the statement into Oswald Bastable's mouth several times in her *Treasure Seekers* (indeed these loved stories may have been one of the sources). What an overwhelming burden if I had to hold that position permanently! I had two younger brothers, Peter then aged eight, and Richard turned two, as well as my mother, now a widow.

My mother came down to see me about three weeks later, a tragic, almost a frightening figure in the full panoply of widow's weeds and unrelieved black, a crêpe veil shrouding her (when it was not lifted) so that she was visibly withdrawn from the world. She had become very pale and very thin, her eyes appearing enormous in her face. All I remember of this visit, besides her appearance, was her asking me where we should spend the summer holidays; and when I said I should like to be in our country house near Windsor, she sighed and said she did not think she could manage it. I realized that this was an

emotional, not a financial statement. This is the only decision I was asked to make, or participate in, then. As a
child I never saw my mother cry.

But if my mother did not then consciously add to the
burden of responsibility I felt and feared, my aunt Nance
did so without scruple. She was my father's only sister, an
emotional, unhappy woman who had had to divorce her
husband (a rare occurrence in those days), with a boy and
a girl of near my age. When I came home for the holidays
she came to the house and somehow got me alone; she
enveloped me in an embrace of black material, burst into
a flood of tears, and pleaded with me to grow up quickly,
to be big and strong like my father, and to look after the
widows and orphans in my charge. My father had helped
her and her children, and she was putting this on me also.
This scene was a traumatic one for me, still today a vivid,
painful memory. Within a very few years I was wearing a
black band for Auntie Nance, who died slowly and painfully of cancer, poor woman.

In the summer of 1915, and thereafter, widows in
mourning became increasingly frequent in the streets, so
that Mother no longer stood out in the crowd. She followed scrupulously the customary usage in the modifica-
tion of her outdoor costume, the shortening and abandoning of the veil, the addition of a touch of white at the
proper calendrical moments. It would have been unthink-
able at that date for a respectable woman to do otherwise.
In early 1917, when she could otherwise have worn some
colour, her father died at a ripe age and she had to return to black for a further six months. His funeral was the
first I had ever attended; the sound of the earth on the
coffin impressed me very much, but it was a general melancholy rather than a poignant grief; he had always seemed
to me so very old, with his white hair and beard, that his

actual death made little impression. There was no question of us grandchildren paying our last respects to his corpse; and I never saw a dead body until I was very much older.

In one way my mother was lucky in the time of her widowing. She was a woman of considerable intelligence who had naturally never been allowed to exercise her potentialities; she was born in 1873, and young ladies at that period were not educated. But as the war progressed, there was an increasing demand for female skills; Mother took the proper courses in what would now be called physiotherapy—massage and the medical use of electricity —and then worked full time at a hospital for wounded soldiers. She also learned to write Braille and transcribed a considerable number of books in the evenings. The emptiness in her life was adequately filled with skilled and useful work. She would not have had such a recourse at any earlier date; she would not have had the support of the ritual of mourning, which freed her from many tedious decisions, very much later.

I cannot from my own memory recall when the full panoply of public mourning became exceptional, rather than general; but the evidence suggests that it was towards the end of the war, in 1917 and 1918. It was not much later that I heard, in one of the first musical comedies I ever saw—called, I think, *Yes, Uncle*—a song which shocked me then, and, on recollection, shocks me still, which began:

> 'Widows are wonderful,
> You must admit they're wise . . .'

One can see the point, of course. The holocaust of young men had created such an army of widows; it was no longer socially realistic for them all to act as though their emotional and sexual life were over for good, which was the underlying message of the ritual mourning. And with the underlying message, the ritual too went into the discard. There was too, almost certainly, a question of public morale; one should not show the face of grief to the boys home on leave from the trenches.

During the latter part of the war I was deeply conscious of the lengthening casualty lists on the front pages of *The Times*. As it happened, nobody close to me was killed; but I had cousins and an uncle at the front, and so in peril, names to be looked for daily; and the war seemed such a permanent condition of life that when I went to Charterhouse at the age of thirteen, I was making rational calculations of the few years likely to remain to me. The armistice was signed during my first term, without forewarning as far as I was concerned, for I had fallen ill with the 'Asian flu' epidemic which was sweeping the world. In my weakened state I burst into tears of relief, much more convulsive than any tears of grief I had ever shed. To this day, I cannot watch a theatrical or cinematographic representation of Armistice Night in London (which of course I did not witness) without breaking into tears.

With the armistice, my preoccupation with and expectation of death diminished, virtually disappeared; so too did my experience of death. My maternal grandmother died a year or so later, during term-time; my mother was indignant that I was not allowed to go to her funeral; but I only recollect a faint sorrow. I wore a black armband for Grannie for three months.

Quite a few years later a sister of my mother was killed in a motor accident while taking a holiday in Spain. Mother fainted when she was told the news over the telephone; but I had only had very intermittent contact with

Auntie Bessie in recent years (she seemed to me to have been cast in the same mould as Lady Catherine de Bourgh) and I do not remember feeling any grief.

I saw a dead body for the first time in 1931, purely by accident, in a hospital in the U.S.S.R. My brother Peter and I had (rather adventurously for the time) gone on an Intourist tour of most of European Russia; and, since he was just qualified as a doctor, he was particularly interested in visiting hospitals. At Kiev, as I recall, the naked corpse of a young woman was carried past us on a rough stretcher. I was startled; and Peter reproached himself that he had not foreseen the possibility of such a confrontation. The picture remains vivid in my mind to this day; she had been a very beautiful girl. But it was only by an effort of imagination that I could conceive that she had ever been alive; the corpse was a *thing*; only intellectually did I realize that it had once been a person.

Three years later I saw, and smelt, a second dead body among the Goro, a tribe in the equatorial forest of the Ivory Coast. I described this incident and the mourning ritual which accompanied the young hunter's lying in state and burial in some detail in the final section of *Africa Dances*.

The outbreak of the Second World War was violently redintegrative of all the gloom and apprehension that I had felt during my childhood, even though I was intellectually convinced that the war was a necessary one; the actual British declaration of war (which I heard over the radio in Mexico City) and the day when Paris fell are two of the most melancholy in my life. I was fortunate in that, although many of my friends and most of my family were in peril, only one friend was killed during the whole of the war—a promising young American classical scholar, Erling Olsen. For me, the Second World War was far less traumatic than the First. I was very busy; and I thought that quite a lot of the work was useful.

My brother Peter married for the first time during the war and lost his wife (from undiagnosed tuberculosis) on the day that the armistice was signed. I never met her; but when I returned to England later in the year Peter's melancholy, emaciation and relative apathy demonstrated vividly the profound physiological and psychological modifications of the personality which deep mourning produced. I did not consciously, at that time, make a connection between the prolongation of his mourning and the lack of any social ritual to ease it. I thought in the conventional terms of a change of scene as a cure (or palliative) for the desolation of grief. I arranged for him to come to the United States, first for a holiday and then to work; this was eventually effective, and he found his second wife there.

I was more conscious of the lack of support which contemporary British society gives to the bereaved when I visited Olive S. in the spring of 1948. Her husband John, one of my very good friends, had died unnecessarily from a cancer of the throat, undiagnosed until the terminal stage; and Olive was left with three young children, the youngest a babe in arms. When I went to see her some two months after John's death, she told me, with tears of gratitude, that I was the first man to stay in the house since she had become a widow. She was being given some good professional help from lawyers and the like who were also friends; but socially she had been almost completely abandoned to loneliness, although the town was full of acquaintances who considered themselves friends.

My mother was starting to turn senile and during the last four years of her life—she died in 1954—degenerated into a helpless, incontinent and almost completely in-

coherent parody of a human being, one of the most distressing transformations one could witness; her death,
when it finally came, was consciously seen as a release
and a relief. Intellectually, I had never quite forgiven her
for having so overburdened my childhood and adolescence
with responsibility; but I wept for her after her cremation.
She had been dying over so long a time that the chief
difference her actual death made was the abandonment
of the flat in which she had spent the last years of her life
and the distribution between my brothers and myself of
the family chattels. Apart from the gathering at the cremation service and letters of condolence there was no
social ritual.

In the same decade her two surviving brothers and one
of her two surviving sisters also died in the fullness of
age; I was not much attached to either of my uncles or my
aunt and felt little grief for them; I did feel some irritation that one of my uncles and my aunt had made me an
executor of their wills without consulting me or getting
my consent. All three were unmarried, and all three were
cremated with the minimum of elaboration.

In 1955, I had put into words my awareness that death
had superseded sex as a taboo subject and one surrounded
with a morbid and furtive fascination for many people,
according to the evidence of the horror comic and the
'X' film; I called my essay The Pornography of Death.[1]
I had also explored in some detail the beliefs about the
afterlife held by a considerable cross-section of English
people[2] and had documented the virtual disappearance
of the beliefs in judgment or damnation or of any of
the terrors which, the evidence suggests, made the fear

[1] See Appendix Four.
[2] Exploring English Character, 1955, Chapter XIV. This topic is
reconsidered in this book, Chapter Two and Appendix Three.

of death so poignant to believing Christians in former generations. Although a variety of unorthodox beliefs about the afterlife were voiced, they were predominantly bland.

When I had wound up all the estates for which I was executor at the beginning of 1960 it seemed as though my personal preoccupation with the sequels to death had, as far as one could foresee, come to a halt; nor were my scientific interests then further directed to the subject.

Then, in April, 1961, Dr. X, who had been a friend and colleague of my brother since they were medical students together, telephoned me the appalling news that Peter, who had gone for a medical check-up because of slight pains in his right shoulder, had been diagnosed as suffering from irremediable cancer: not only were his lungs affected (from a child he had suffered much from bronchitis and asthma) but also his spine; the prognosis was absolutely hopeless, a probable twelve months of increasing debility and pain before an agonized death. He asked me to decide whether his wife, Elizabeth, should be informed; he had already decided to hide the truth from Peter; and he and his colleagues engaged in the most elaborate and successful medical mystification to hide from Peter's expert knowledge the facts of their diagnosis.

I was emotionally completely unprepared. I had (have) long believed that I was likely to die of cancer, since my father's parents and his brother and sister had all died of cancer and a brother of my mother of leukemia; I had accepted that I carried a diseased inheritance. But, quite illogically, I had never intellectually considered that my brothers had the same inheritance as myself, perhaps in part because I resemble my father in features and colouring, whereas Peter and Richard took much more after my mother's family. It is probable too that, in the same way that I had intellectually accepted responsibility for my mother and brothers after my father's death, I had unconsciously thought that I would take the burden of our cancerous heredity away from the others.

Peter was at the happiest and most successful period of his life, blissfully married and enjoying his two children, innocently delighted with his election as a Fellow of the Royal Society and the growing international recognition of his scientific work, and looking forward to having his own department created for him. In the 1930's, when I had a certain success as a writer, he was frequently asked whether he was related to me; in the last years of his life I was being asked whether I was related to him.

The fact that he was engaged in very original scientific work added extra qualms to my collusion in the kindly meant deception that his colleagues at Guy's Hospital were practising on him. I felt sure that, under similar circumstances, I should wish to be informed so that, if at all possible, the scientific ideas and unrealized projects could be transmitted to others to carry through; we shared a respect for the values of scientific knowledge which I felt were being transgressed. Further, I foresaw (for my wartime work had taught me the burden of secrets) that my relationship to him, and that of anybody else so informed, would be progressively falsified by the inevitable continuous dissimulation. I fully intended to argue about the ethics of such deception with Dr. X at a slightly later date; but he and his colleagues had persuaded Peter that he was run down and slightly arthritic and needed a good holiday; and I was willing that he should have this relatively carefree period.

Whether Elizabeth should be informed was a much more pressing and perplexing problem. The knowledge would, I knew, reduce her to despair, for she was com-

pletely devoted to Peter; apart from her garden she had
no interests which were not also his, her English friends
and acquaintances were almost all his colleagues and
their spouses.

In my perplexity I consulted Dr. Y. He is the wisest
British man I know concerning human relations (our
mutual friend and my former collaborator, the late Dr.
John Rickman, was such another), and I thought that he
would see the situation more clearly than I could in my
deep distress; by good fortune he and his wife were coming to see me some four days after I had spoken to Dr.
X. His advice was that Elizabeth should be told; one of
the arguments he advanced was that, if she were ignorant, she might show impatience or lack of understanding
with his probably increasing weakness, for which she
would reproach herself later; she could use the final
months of their marriage better if she knew them for
what they were. That night, and for many months afterwards, I cried myself to sleep, rather noisy sobs.

Elizabeth was told by Dr. X, and took the terrible news
with magnificent courage and common sense. Her role in
the deception was infinitely harder than mine, for she
could never let up, never safely abandon herself to grief; I
doubt if she could have supported the continuous pretence for long.

It was arranged that, on his discharge from Guy's, Peter
and Elizabeth should come and spend a week with me in
the country, and then go on to Blagdon for some fishing,
a pastime to which Peter was passionately addicted. He
breakfasted in bed, and rose late, but otherwise he seemed
in the highest of spirits, indeed rather euphoric; he was
continuously elaborating plans for a future which Elizabeth and I knew he would never see. I thought the eu-
phoria might in part be due to the analgesics of which

Dr. X had given him a considerable supply; but Elizabeth did not think so.

In the evening of May 10th, 1961, I had a dinner engagement in London which I kept; when I returned home a little before midnight Peter and Elizabeth were still up, happy and mellow. We went to bed rather late. In the morning when their breakfast was brought to them Elizabeth rushed into my room, saying Peter was either in a coma or dead. He was very clearly dead, his face cyanosed and his body cooling. Elizabeth collapsed into my bed.

The rest of the day was a busy nightmare, though I could find at least intellectual comfort in the knowledge that Peter had been spared the increasing pain and weakness which the prognosis had foreseen; he had died in his sleep, without any signs of pain, from what the autopsy showed to have been oedema of the lung. An autopsy was necessary, since he had died away from home and was to be cremated; my doctor, kind Dr. Z, whom I had summoned immediately, gave all the help he could; but a cremation certificate could not be granted without the presence of Dr. X, and he was unable to come down.

Dr. Z got in touch with the undertakers for me, and it was arranged for a pair of ex-nurses to come to lay out the body. They imparted a somewhat Dickensian tone; they were fat and jolly, and asked in a respectful but cheerful tone, 'Where is the patient?' One of them was out a couple of minutes later to ask if he had a fresh pair of pyjamas; I could not bring myself to go through his clothes, and showed them his suitcase. Some half-hour later their work was done, and they came out saying, 'The patient looks lovely now. Come and have a look!' I did not wish to, at which they expressed surprise. I gave them a pound for their pains; the leader, pure Sarah Gamp, said, 'That for us, duck? Cheers!' and went through the motions of raising a bottle and emptying it into her mouth. I sat with Elizabeth when, shortly afterwards, the undertaker's men came to take the body away; the noise of their feet on the uncarpeted stairs was slow and sinister. Later, I had to go to the mortuary to make a formal identification of the corpse, before the autopsy could be made. I was frightened of fainting, for I felt nearly exhausted; I did not, however, though I slumped into a chair as I confirmed that it was my dear brother. The layers-out had done a good job; he was composed, colourless and waxen. The two pictures of his corpse remain completely vivid in my memory.

Besides all the problems connected with the disposal of the body, there were many people to be informed of his death, and complicated arrangements to be made to tell the children of their father's death and arrange for them to come to me. These arrangements Elizabeth thought out with great clarity; she was completely prostrate—it was hours before she felt strong enough to walk across the hall to another room I had had prepared for her; and I also had to tidy up their previous room and pack away Peter's clothes and belongings into a suitcase, lest their sight distress Elizabeth, or the children who would occupy the room on the morrow. Although I was crying much of the time while I performed these tasks, it was only in the evening, when Elizabeth was hopefully sleeping under sedation, that the full extent of our loss overwhelmed me. The situation was damnably redintegrative; here I was again, responsible for a widow and two young children.

Owing to the necessity of an autopsy, there was a longer delay than customary between Peter's death and his cremation; the interval passed in a daze, interrupted with bouts of busyness for me. The weather was wonderful, and nearly all the daylight hours were spent out of doors, with picnics in the garden or the fields. Elizabeth decided not to come to the cremation herself— she could not bear the thought that she might lose control and other people observe her grief; and she wished to spare the children the distressing experience. As a consequence, their father's death was quite unmarked for them by any ritual of any kind, and was even nearly treated as a secret, for it was very many months before Elizabeth could bear to mention him or have him mentioned in her presence.

In his will, Peter had requested a Church of England service for his cremation, I presume because this would cause the least trouble; none of us had any sort of religious belief. Neither of the clergymen who were personal friends was available to conduct the service; the crematorium supplied a handsome cleric, dressed in a sky-blue robe, with dramatic, even theatrical, gestures. The moment, in a cremation service, when the coffin disappears through the folding doors still seems (despite frequent exposure) a moment of the most poignant finality. Many of Peter's friends and nearly all our surviving relatives were present.

The only time that I felt near to collapsing was on the return from the cremation (it involved a two-hour motordrive each way); I had to go to bed, to be by myself, for a few hours. With enormous courage, Elizabeth assured me that she and the children had had a good day; they had taken a picnic to the fields where the grass was being cut for silage. All the people who worked for me treated us all with the greatest thoughtfulness and consideration, a gentle kindness which was really comforting.

We all went for a few days to friends in Frome; and then life had to be resumed. It was the experience of the following months which suggested to me that our treatment of grief and mourning made bereavement very difficult to be lived through.

In my own case, I was able to mourn freely, to indulge in passionate bouts of weeping without self-reproach. I lost about twenty pounds in weight over the following three months, and my sleep tended to be disturbed. I had frequent dreams of Peter, many of them about our early childhood; waking from them was very distressing. I did all the routine work necessary, but felt disinclined for anything which demanded prolonged concentration. I wore a black tie for about three months. I had great pleasure in seeing real friends, but was unwilling to meet strangers. A couple of times I refused invitations to cocktail parties, explaining that I was mourning; the people who invited me responded to this statement with shocked embarrassment, as if I had voiced some appalling obscenity. Indeed, I got the impression that, had I stated that the invitation clashed with some esoteric debauchery I had arranged, I would have had understanding and jocular encouragement; as it was, the people whose invitations I had refused, educated and sophisticated though they were, mumbled and hurried away. They clearly no longer had any guidance from ritual as to the way to treat a self-confessed mourner; and, I suspect, they were frightened lest I give way to my grief, and involve them in a distasteful upsurge of emotion.

This would certainly seem to be the explanation of the way in which Elizabeth was avoided by her and Peter's friends; they treated her, she said, as though she were a leper. Only if she acted as though nothing of consequence had happened was she again socially acceptable.

This fear of the expression of grief on the part of the

English professional classes unfortunately matched Elizabeth's New England fear of giving way to grief, of losing self-control. She did not wear black clothes nor ritualize her mourning in any way; she let herself be, almost literally, eaten up with grief, sinking into a deep and long-lasting depression. At the period when she most needed help and comfort from society she was left alone.

As an anthropologist, I knew that the vast majority of recorded human societies have developed formal rituals for mourning. Typically there are communal ceremonies from the period immediately after the death until the disposal of the body; typically, the bereaved are distinguished by a change in their physical appearance, such as special clothes, shaving the hair or letting it grow and so on, so that all who come into contact with them know they are mourners and treat them in a specified ritualistic fashion; and, typically, a mourner goes through what van Gennep called a *rite de passage*—a formal withdrawal from society, a period of seclusion, and a formal re-entry into society.

If a custom, such as this, is very widespread throughout human societies at all stages of development, it seems reasonable to assume that the custom is congruent with species-characteristic human psychology; and, as a corollary, those aberrant societies which lack such a custom are failing to provide their members with the support which most societies make available. The absence of such support in the professional middle classes in southern England was, as I have described, brought forcibly to my attention in the months following Peter's death; but before I made generalizations and drew conclusions from my own experience and that of those recently bereaved people whom I chanced to meet and could question, it

seemed desirable to make a survey and conduct interviews among all classes and in all regions of Britain. The
chapters that follow describe the findings of this survey
and interviews.

CHAPTER ONE

A DEATH IN THE FAMILY

i The Bereaved

During the month of May, 1963, a carefully selected sample of 1,628 people of both sexes, of all ages over 16, coming from every social class and every region of Britain were asked: 'Have you ever attended a funeral or cremation?' Some 15 per cent of these, predominantly young people under 34, had never done so. The remainder who had attended such a ceremony were asked when they had last attended such a ceremony, and who it was for? Thirty per cent of the total had last attended such a ceremony more than five years previously; since it was likely that their recollections of the event would not be very vivid, they were not questioned further; this left 903 people who had attended a funeral service within the last five years.

Out of this total 240 (just over a quarter) had paid their respects to a person not related in any way; 186 (a fifth) had attended the funeral of an in-law, and exactly the same number had attended the funeral of a secondary relative—grandparents, uncles, aunts, cousins and one grandchild. These people were asked if they had also attended the funeral of any member of their immediate family in the last five years? Forty-three had lost a parent, 20 a brother or sister, 12 a spouse and 1 a child during that period; these were added to the 290 people who had mentioned a close relative in the first instance. Seven of these people were not willing to answer any further questions about their bereavement; the remaining 359 constitute the main sample which is discussed in the following pages. One hundred and ninety-two of these people had lost a parent, 86 a brother or a sister, 66 a husband or wife and 15 a child in the previous five years. I re-interviewed, at considerably greater length, 80 of these mourners; of these 13 had lost a father and 14 a mother, 23 a husband, 9 a wife, 7 a brother, 8 a sister and 6 a child who had passed infancy.[1]

Precisely half the deaths in the major sample had taken place in hospital; of the remainder, 44 per cent had died at home and the rest had died elsewhere. It would seem, therefore, that to die in one's own bed is becoming slightly exceptional.[2]

The main sample were not asked about the cause of death; out of the 80 whom I interviewed, 16 reported death from a coronary attack (frequently without any previous warning) and 19 from cancer. In nearly all the latter cases, the survivor was told by the doctor or hospital that their relative was incurable; but without exception the dying man or woman was kept in ignorance.

Now that cancer is becoming so common a cause of death, the ethics of this habitual medical practice might usefully be reconsidered. I presume that the rationalization for lying to the patient and forcing his or her spouse or children or other relatives into a conspiracy of deceit is that, if the patient were told, he or she might give way to despair and slightly shorten his life by committing sui-

[1] The reasons for which, and the methods by which, these 80 were chosen out of the larger sample are discussed in Appendix Two.
[2] This seems to be the case in the United States also. See *The Meaning of Death*, edited by Dr. Herman Feifel (New York, 1955), pp. 120 ff.

cide.[3] Against this possible risk is the undoubted fact that the whole relationship between the dying and their partners or close relatives is falsified and distorted in a particularly degrading and painful fashion.

To illustrate this, I will quote from two widows in the Midlands.[4] A middle-aged miner's widow said (1):

'I knew he was dying, but he didn't. It didn't sink in, the doctor told me, but I just couldn't grasp. . . . It was terrible having to lie to him; I had to be cruel really. I was abrupt with him sort of, or I would have broke down.'

The 49-year-old widow of a man who worked in retail distribution (2):

[3] As far as my knowledge goes, the only recent consideration of this problem in medical ethics and human psychology occurs in two of the papers of *The Meaning of Death* (see previous footnote). Dr. August M. Kasper's paper, *The Doctor and Death*, considers with great insight the doctor's inevitable ambivalence towards a dying patient; and Dr. Herman Feifel in *The Attitudes Towards Death in some Normal and Mentally Ill Populations* states that his experience indicates that it is helpful to the dying to discuss their situation. 'I think one of the serious mistakes we commit in treating terminally ill patients is the erection of a psychological barrier between the living and the dying. Some think and say it is cruel and traumatic to talk to dying patients about death. Actually, my findings indicate that patients want very much to talk about their feelings and thoughts about death, but feel that we, the living, close off the avenues for their accomplishing this. . . . A goodly number of terminally ill patients prefer honest and plain talk about the seriousness of their illness from their physicians. . . . Some of them actually thanked the project personnel for affording them the opportunity to discuss their feeling concerning death. . . . It seems that in many circumstances it is not *what* the patient is told but rather *how* it is done that counts . . ." (pp. 123–125).
The thanks of the dying patients recorded by Dr. Feifel are paralleled by the gratitude expressed by many of my informants for talking to them about their grief. See p. 128.
[4] To preserve my respondents' anonymity, I am only stating the region from which they come and, where relevant, their occupation. In Appendix Two I list all the areas in which interviews took place.

'He was ill for 22 months with cancer. I knew, but he didn't. . . . It was a great strain; I'd break down when he was upstairs. Now I think: "Did I do right not to tell him?" . . . My husband was always talking about what he was going to do. It was very hard. They thought my husband would die sooner, but he lingered on; his courage was tremendous. It's very difficult, and you think after if you did right. He used to ask me if he was going to get well, and I often wonder if I did right. My doctor said *he* wasn't going to tell him, and the hospital wouldn't either; so if I tell him, he's not going to have much faith in the hospital, is he? It's just one of those things. I told him awful lies.'

These two informants are typical of many. What had been good marriages (as the remainder of the interviews show) were reduced to unkindness or falsity by the doctor's professional (or, one might think in the second case, pusillanimous) unwillingness to tell his patient the truth. It would obviously be harrowing for a doctor to have to do so, and it is understandable that they share the British fear of the display of emotion; but it would seem worth considering whether this practice is not causing avoidable misery. One woman said that her mother had committed suicide by gassing herself because (as she stated in the note she left) she could not bear the burden of the secret that her husband was dying of cancer.

It looks as if the pattern of dying is changing. The younger the bereaved respondent, the more likely he or she is to report the death in hospital; but the figures are not sufficient to make sure this is a significant change. By a relatively small figure, more parents are reported as dying at home than spouses or siblings. Deaths at home are significantly more common in the families of clerical workers and unskilled workers, in small towns of between 50,000–100,000 inhabitants and in the Midlands. Nearly two-thirds of Scottish deaths occur in hospital. Members nominally of the Church of England are more likely to die at home than are adherents to other sects; Roman Catholics have a markedly high proportion of deaths in hospital.

Most people, it would seem, now die alone, except for medical attendants; less than a quarter of the bereaved were present when their relative died, and nearly two-thirds of those present were women. In this situation, as in so many others, the behaviour of those who lost a spouse differs significantly from that of the other bereaved; nearly half of the widowed were present at the death of their partner. A child was present in a quarter of the cases when a parent died; but, with insignificant exceptions, brothers or sisters are absent when their siblings die. Nearly all the children died in hospital, alone.

In the upper middle and professional classes it is rare for the bereaved person to be present at death (less than 1 in 8); as one descends the class structure, presence becomes more common, reaching nearly a third in the unskilled working class. In the regions, such attendance is commonest in Scotland, and least common in the Midlands and the South-East; somewhat ambiguously, it is also least common in towns of 50,000–100,000 inhabitants.

If the evidence of nineteenth-century novelists is to be trusted, the presence of one's closest kin round a death-bed was then general in all ranks of society; the preservation of this custom in the unskilled working classes may be an example of the frequently observed trend of customs to be persisted in by the lower ranks of society for a considerable time after they had been discarded by the middle and upper ranks. Few informants commented on these deathbeds at which they had assisted; but when they did it seems as if the experience is comforting. The elderly wife of an unskilled worker from the South-East (3) said that her mother and her eldest sister had died in her arms, and now she has no fear of death at all; a retired stoker from the Midlands (4) said of his wife:

'When I see her die she looked like she was going to a place where she would be happy. She smiled.'

Another custom which has been preserved much more widely in the working classes than in the middle classes is that of paying one's respect to the body after death and before the funeral. Two-thirds of the bereaved, in all, had followed this ritual; in the unskilled working class the proportion rose to over three-quarters; in the upper middle and professional classes it fell to under half. Men perform this rite somewhat more than women (but women are more frequently present at the deathbed). This custom varies little with the age of the mourner. It is nearly universal in the North-West (nearly all Roman Catholics perform this rite as part of the wake) and uncommon in the Midlands and South-West.

For some informants this viewing of the body seems to be almost traumatic. The wife of a jobbing gardener in the South-East (5), who had lost her mother fairly recently and her father some years earlier, said:

'Well, I think a lot of the trouble is now, with my father you see I saw him in the coffin, and I always remembered him in the coffin, but with my mother we were in the hospital when she drew her last breath, and we knew she was going, but we didn't see her after that . . . and it's funny but I never think of *her* in the coffin.'

She further said that she thought that the really important difference between her grief for her father and that for her mother was that she had seen her father in the coffin and never seen her mother cold, and, as a result, she felt that the funeral was a farce, and that her mother is not really dead. She remembers her mother as a live woman, her father as a dead man.

The wife of an assistant sales manager in the Midlands (6), talking about the death of her father in January, 1963:

'They couldn't bury him straight away—that cold January there was a lot waiting you see, and my mother had him till Friday in that front room, we was worried with her by herself so we took it in turns to sleep with her, and before she went to bed each night she went into the front room and kissed him goodnight. It frightened me to death. . . . She would insist that I go too and it upset me. I said: "Oh! where's all his colour gone?" because he was dead white; and she said: "Of course, they go white when they're dead." And that upset me. I dreamt of him every night with his very white face and blue and white pyjamas.'

Similarly, a schoolmaster from Scotland (7) says that in his dreams his mother, who had died the year before, is always very pale.

'I think this may be because I saw her when she was dead, and one of my thoughts was "this deathly pallor", you know.'

Although nearly a third of the respondents did not pay their respects to the body of the relative about whose funeral they were being questioned, all but a small minority (7 per cent of the total) had at some time of their life seen the body of a person who had died a natural death. I was rather surprised at this answer. Three-quarters of the people who have not had this experience are women, mostly under 44, nominally Church of England, and somewhat concentrated in the Midlands. Only two of the widowed fell into this category. Exposure to the physical fact of natural death is much more general than I had anticipated.

ii *The House of Mourning*

Four-fifths of the population continue the traditional custom of indicating to passers-by that there are mourners in the house. Much the most usual token is drawn blinds. This was done for two-thirds of the middle-class homes, and four-fifths of the working classes. There are some regional differences in the observation of this custom. In the North of England it is observed almost universally; and in some homogenous working-class districts (according to two Northern informants) every house in the street will draw its blinds for the period of the funeral, from the time that the coffin leaves the house until the mourners return. This drawing of blinds is reported by less than two-thirds of the respondents in the South-East and by under half in Scotland. In Scotland (and, to a lesser extent, in the northern parts of England) there exists an alternative or supplementary sign in the form of mourning cards. These are similar to greeting cards, but often quite elaborate and embellished with holy pictures and appropriate verses or (for Roman Catholics) prayers; these may be displayed by placing them in a ground-floor window, facing the street, legible to the visitor or passer-by.

These stylized forms of condolence are uncommon

in the Midlands or South of England; in the North and in Scotland their employment is reported more frequently among the skilled clerical and working classes than among the middle classes or the unskilled workers.

For a very small group, predominantly in the North-East, the presence of death in a house is indicated by a wreath of either flowers or evergreens ornamented with white ribbons hung on the street door.

Nearly a third of the professional and clerical classes (as contrasted to nearly a sixth of the working classes) omit all public indications that there are mourners in the house. This absence of signs is most frequent in the South-East, followed by the South-West; it is very infrequent in the North-West, the Midlands and the North. The employment of public indications that there are mourners in the house rises slightly with the age of the respondents; they are more frequently employed for the loss of a spouse or sibling than they are for the loss of a parent.

It is customary for there to be a family gathering at the house before the funeral; this was omitted in less than a fifth of the cases of the total, but, significantly, by nearly a third of the respondents of the professional classes. Such family gatherings were less frequent in Scotland than in any region of England or in Wales, perhaps because of the traditional scattering of Scottish families. But when such family gatherings before the funeral did occur in Scotland they were nearly always accompanied by a religious service in the home (naturally, predominantly services of the Church of Scotland or Roman Catholic); in the rest of the country such services in the home occur in about a quarter of the cases, with the exception of the South-East; there less than one family in ten has a religious ceremony in the home. About half

the respondents who were members of the Roman Catholic Church, the Church of Scotland and the Nonconformist Churches had religious ceremonies in the home;
but less than a sixth of those calling themselves Church
of England. Religious ceremonies in the home were reported more frequently by the younger respondents; they
were least frequent in the middle classes and most frequent in the unskilled working class.

iii Telling the Children

Traditionally, British parents find it embarrassing to
talk to their children on subjects of deep emotional importance; and traditionally they try to hide their own
deep emotions from their children's observation. Consequently, it seemed useful to ask all parents of children
under sixteen what they had told them about death. They
nearly all interpreted this question as referring to the
recent bereavement on which they were being questioned.
They were also asked if this was more or less the same
as they were told when they were young, and, if not, in
what way this was different?

A little over a third of the respondents, 126 in all, had
children under 16; 56 of these—just under a half—for
one reason or another, some of them valid, did not tell
their children anything at all, nor discuss the subject with
them. Of the remainder, 35 told their children the truth
as they saw it; 42 employed some form of euphemism.

The most prevalent of the religious euphemisms are
'gone to heaven', 'gone to Jesus' and the like; and what
is noteworthy is that these religious euphemisms are frequently employed by people who seem to have no religious convictions themselves, who state explicitly that
they do not believe in an afterlife, never go to a place of

worship or say private prayers. It is difficult to avoid the
conclusion that a sizeable minority of British parents are
using God and Jesus in communication with their children in exactly the same way as they use Santa Claus—as
fairy-tale figures.

An intelligent 36-year-old writer from the South-East
(8) who had recently lost his mother, was particularly
articulate about this problem.

> 'One of the difficulties when she died,' *he said*, 'and
> this may be a common problem, is knowing what to
> tell the children. We told them that she'd died; my
> conscience would have been easier if I had told them
> that we didn't know what had happened to her then;
> but I was rather cowardly about this and told them
> that she had gone to heaven. . . . Actually to where
> she came from before she was born. . . . Well, you
> see, it's such a useful thing to have. It is difficult be-
> cause children are upset by death and they want to
> know what has happened. It's quite a difficult one to
> deal with. I've noticed that since then our daughter
> has been frightened of dying; it's come out occasionally.
> It's quite a difficult thing to explain to a child. . . . I
> think it's difficult for me, because I was brought up in
> a religious background. One feels slightly dishonest
> about it.'

One mother, the wife of an accountant in the South-
East (9), actually used the metaphor of a fairy story:

> 'I told her that Grandad had gone to Jesus in heaven.
> I tried to make it as much like a fairy story as possible,
> without telling lies.'

This mother expressed a belief in the afterlife, and is a
fairly regular churchgoer; but the following typical par-

ents are not churchgoers, seldom or never say prayers; the six first quoted say they have no belief in an afterlife, the remainder that they are uncertain.

The 35-year-old wife of a steel-welder from the Midlands, Church of England:

'I told the children that Grandad had gone to heaven.'

The 36-year-old wife of a staff-sergeant from Scotland, Church of Scotland:

'My two eldest children understood what was happening without being told, and my friend explained to my youngest one that Grandma had gone to heaven and would come back in another form.'

A 34-year-old building labourer from the South-East, Church of England:

'I just told them he had gone to heaven.'

A 35-year-old business-manager from the North-West, Church of England:

'We told them that she had died and we attended the funeral. The two youngest ones just accepted it, but Stephen, the eldest, was more upset. We just spoke about dying and about God, and that was it.'

A 40-year-old skilled labourer from the North-East, Church of England:

'I told them that Auntie Norah had died and gone to heaven with Grandma and that he would not see her again.'

A 32-year-old general labourer from the North-West, Roman Catholic:

'I just said that his sister had gone to heaven.'

A 50-year-old tailor's cutter from the North-East (10):

'The elder one understood but I told the younger one that Grandma had gone to heaven—he wanted to know when she was coming back. I told him she was staying with God.'

A 36-year-old widow from Scotland, Church of England:

'I told them Daddy had died, that God must have wanted him.'

I count this statement a euphemism, since the respondent said earlier that she never went to church nor said private prayers, and had no belief in an afterlife. In contrast, another widow, 45-year-old, from Scotland (11) who told her children that 'Daddy had gone to Jesus' is counted among the very few who gave their children what may be called a factual religious explanation. This respondent goes to Church of England services every week and says daily prayers; the children could see a congruence between their mother's regular behaviour and the explanation she gave them of their father's death, which would surely have been missing in the earlier respondents quoted.

Besides the euphemisms employing the religious phrases, there are the customary verbal euphemisms tending to deny the fact of death—'gone to sleep', 'gone to rest' and the like. One which seems to be frequently used is to tell the children that the dead grandparent, uncle or aunt has gone away on a long visit; this seems a particularly unfortunate phrasing. Examples are a 46-year-old school-teacher from Scotland (7):

'We told my son quietly that his Granny had gone away.'

A 40-year-old teacher from the South-East, Church of England:

'We told them that Nan had gone away for a long holiday and will not come back. She has gone to stay with Baby Jesus.'

A 38-year-old motor mechanic from the North-East, a Methodist who says he does not believe in an afterlife:

'We told him that Grandmother had gone to heaven where he wanted to go and see her.'

A 44-year-old tool-fitter from Scotland (12):

'I told my younger son that Grandad was in a long sleep and was gone away to a happy land.'

A 56-year-old cleaning inspector from London, Church of England:

'I just told them that Nanny had just gone to sleep, you won't see her again.'

A 34-year-old building foreman from the South-East (13):

'The wife had already told them that when people died they are with the angels and they know from books and pictures that the angels are supposed to watch over them and keep them from harm.'

A third of our parents told their children the secular facts with relatively little embroidery; thus the 35-year-old wife of a male nurse from the South-East, a member of the Argyll Hall Brethren:

'I never tell them lies—I told them that Grandma was dead and what she died of, and they could go to her grave every Sunday.'

The 49-year-old wife of a director of a small firm in the South-East (14):

'They have been brought up to know that death comes to all of us when it is time and as new people are born some are already due to die or else there would not be room for everybody here.'

A 41-year-old antique dealer from the South-West (15), a practising Methodist:

'I explained that Grandpa had died. I think they understood death from seeing animals, etc., die and understand that a person just goes.'

The 38-year-old wife of a retail distributor from the Midlands Church of England:

'I told them the truth—that their Nanna was so ill and when people were so ill for a very long time they did not usually get better when they were getting old.'

The 37-year-old wife of a railway clerk from the North-East (16), Church of England:

'I explained that Grandmother was very tired and had gone to sleep. The girl of twelve already knew about people dying. Her younger sister accepted that and never asked any questions.'

A 37-year-old wife of a wharf merchant from the South-East, Church of England:

'We just told her that Grandpa had collapsed and died and she more or less understood it.'

A 36-year-old engineer from the North-East, Church of England:

'I just told them it was natural causes that had caused my brother's death.'

The 47-year-old wife of a jobbing gardener from the South-East (5), Church of England:

'I told them that Granny had died and was buried in a nice garden and that we could go and take flowers there and keep it looking nice.'

The 41-year-old wife of a Midlands sales manager (6):

'I just told them that Grandad had died, that was all. Being teenagers they don't worry about things like that these days.'

The reply last quoted shades into the more reputable reasons for telling children nothing about the death in the family (an attitude adopted by 44 per cent of the respondents)—these concern the age of the child, either old enough to be probably aware of the facts of death, or too young to understand. Thus a 37-year-old fire officer from the North-East, Church of England:

'There is nothing much you can tell them at that age, just below sixteen and grammar-school educated.'

But, time and again, there is just evasion of the subject. A 48-year-old part-time barmaid from the North-East (17):

'I told him that his Grandad was in hospital. I think he knows now but I didn't tell him.'

Sometimes the lack of explanation is reasonable. The 55-year-old wife of a Midlands professional man (18) said:

'She already knew about death, there was nothing to tell her. She has been brought up on these lines, joining in conversations; we talked to her like one of us.'

A 40-year-old schoolmaster from the South-East who had lost a child in an accident said of his daughter:

'It was so sudden and such a shock, there was no time to tell her anything. She was not frightened when the body lay in the house, but on the other hand she did not take a morbid interest.'

More typical is a 38-year-old driving instructor from the South-East, a Methodist:

'I told them nothing. They have never asked.'

The 39-year-old wife of a plasterer from the South-East, Church of England:

'I did not explain. I expect they got it from school.'

A 47-year-old fire-officer from the North-West, nominal Church of England, who had lost a sister:

'I did not let them take any part in the proceedings, and as I was not asked told them nothing.'

This treatment of death as a literally unmentionable subject (and it seems to be the commonest of all approaches)[5] would seem to be capable of having a number of undesirable consequences. A 45-year-old widow in Scotland (11), whose husband had collapsed and died of a heart attack while on a family picnic said of her children that the girl was average in school, but the boy, the next one, 'was having a struggle with everything. It was him that found his father.' This boy never mentioned his ter-

[5] Similar evasions are recounted by Peter Marris in *Widows and their Families*, pp. 36–38.

rifying experience, and his mother would not (could not bear to) talk about it to him, and was apparently unwilling for anyone else to do so. I think there is little doubt that this boy was severely traumatized by the treatment of his experience as unmentionable; I was told of two other not dissimilar cases. I have argued elsewhere that this secrecy is in large part responsible for the furtive excitement engendered by horror comics and some 'X' films —the 'pornography of death'.

My attempt to discover through the questionnaire whether today's parents were using the same explanations about death to their children as they had received in their own childhood was not successful, as over a third of the respondents did not answer this question, typically because they could not remember. Just under a half think that they were giving the same explanations as they had received; and just under a quarter that they were giving different explanations.

No clear pattern is discernible in these changes. Those who give their children realistic explanations say that they were fobbed off with religious euphemisms, those who use euphemisms say that they were given the bare facts crudely. 'When I was a child I was told plainly that my grandmother was dead,' said a Scottish school-teacher (7). More typical is the statement of the wife of a railway clerk in the North-East (16):

'When I was a child I was never told anything about it at all. At home I was thirteen when my Granny died, and I cannot remember being told anything.'

Two informants, both of them sincerely religious people, think that the treatment of death is easier for children now than it was a generation ago. The wife of a director of a small firm in the South-East (14), who had recently lost her adoptive mother to whom she was devoted, said:

'I think people do accept death far easier now than they did when I was a child. If anybody passed on when I was a child everything was hush-hush and everybody looked so sorrowful and mournful and you were hardly allowed to whisper; well, I think all that has died out. It's the acceptance that one doesn't have to be miserable to mourn. . . . You must sort of hide your feelings for those around you; when you're on your own and think about those you've lost you do your mourning quietly, alone. The same as you might do praying.'

An antique dealer from the South-West (15) said:

'People are more frank about birth and death nowadays and do not embroider the facts.'

Unfortunately, this research does not bear him out.

CHAPTER TWO

RELIGION AND THE BEREAVED

i Denominations

It is very rare indeed in Britain for a dead body to be disposed of without benefit of clergy. In the sample of 359 there were only two cases of 'non-denominational' services; in 13 other cases the answers are obscure; the remaining 344 funerals or cremations were accompanied by religious rites. In no other area of British life has re-

ligion such a near monopoly. Many infants are not chris-
tened (even outside the sects which do not employ infant
baptism) but merely have their births registered; many
marriages take place in registry offices; but death is a religious preserve.

Because religion impinges on more British people in
early bereavement than on any other occasion in their
lives, because all versions of Christianity contain dogmatic statements about the reality of a life after death
and its nature, and because, traditionally, religion is held
to offer consolations for the grief of bereavement, I decided that the sample of mourners should be asked the
same questions as had been answered by the much larger
and more heterogenous samples reported on in *Exploring
English Character*.[1]
These questions are:

   (i)   Would you describe yourself as being of any re-
        ligion or denomination? If yes, which?
  (ii)   How often do you normally attend a church
        service?
 (iii)   Do you ever say any private prayers? How often?
 (iv)   Do you believe in the Devil?
  (v)   Do you believe in an afterlife? If yes, what will
        it be like?

Six per cent—15 men and 8 women—denied having any
religious denomination; these were predominantly people
under 44, and concentrated in the South-East and Midlands; there were none in the North-West, and only 3
in the North-East and Scotland. With the exception of a
solitary Jew and 7 Spiritualists, Christian Scientists and

[1] The contrasts and similarities between these two samples, the
one taken in 1950, the second in 1963, are analysed in Appendix
Three. In general, the resemblances are far more striking than the
differences.

other members of modern sects, all the remainder claimed membership of some Christian sect.

Far and away the largest group, with 61 per cent, call themselves Church of England; these are followed by 11 per cent Roman Catholic, 8 per cent each of Church of Scotland and Methodists, and very small groups of Baptists, Congregationalists and 'Christians'. (Because the figures are so small, members of the five last-mentioned sects are grouped together as 'Nonconformists' in some analyses.)

Members of the Church of England are heavily concentrated in the South-East and the Midlands and are a minority in Scotland; they are concentrated in towns of between 50,000–100,000 inhabitants. They are, by a little, most numerous in the middle and professional classes and least numerous among skilled clerical workers (who have a high proportion of Methodists). Only three members of the Church of Scotland live outside Scotland; within that country they are evenly represented among all ages and social classes. The Roman Catholics represent over a quarter of the respondents from the North-West and are relatively numerous in the North-East and in Scotland; they belong overwhelmingly to the working classes, and in these classes to the least skilled. They are predominantly urban. It is perhaps relevant that out of the 15 children whose death was mourned, 8 were of Roman Catholic parentage. Adherents to the smaller Nonconformist groups tend to come from the villages and towns of less than 50,000 inhabitants in the South of the island. All but one of the adherents to the modern cults are women.

In general, the women among the bereaved are much more regular in their public and private devotions than are the men. Two-thirds of the women, but only a quarter of the men, say private prayers daily or more frequently; nearly half the men, but barely an eighth of the women, never say any prayers at all. The contrast is less marked in church-going; 14 per cent of the men and 21 per cent of the women go to their place of worship weekly or more frequently; 39 per cent of the men and 31 per cent of the women go to their place of worship on special occasions only, weddings, funerals and the like. Seventeen per cent of both sexes say that they never enter a place of worship at all.

The younger the respondents the less likely they are to say regular private prayers; less than a quarter of those under 35 do so, as contrasted with three-fifths of those over 55. This pattern is much less marked in attendance at public places of worship; the minority (less than a third of the total) who go to church or chapel once a month or more frequently are evenly distributed among all the age groups.

The social make-up of the congregations is predominantly upper middle class and lower working class; a small proportion (less than a fifth) of the skilled workers are even moderately devout. Three-fifths of this class, if they enter sacred buildings at all, do so only on special occasions; the corresponding figure for the upper middle classes is one-third. A quarter of the members of the upper middle classes never say private prayers, which suggests that some of their church-going may be of formal social significance. The skilled working class contains the lowest proportion of those who say regular private prayers and the highest proportion of those who never pray.

The Roman Catholics are by far the most regular in both their public and private devotions; three-fifths of them go to church once a week or more often, in contrast with 25 per cent of the Church of Scotland and

the Nonconformists, and 9 per cent of those who call
themselves Church of England. Just under half of the
Nonconformists and well over half of the members of
the Church of England never go to church or chapel at
all, or only on special occasions; for the Roman Catholics
the figure is less than a quarter. A third of the members
of the Church of England and the Nonconformists
never say private prayers at all, or only in peril or grief; the
corresponding figure for the Roman Catholics is 8 per
cent.

Since the Roman Catholics are concentrated in the
North-West and in Scotland these areas have much the
highest figures for regular church attendance, and London and the South-East much the lowest; but the converse is not quite exact. The South-West and Scotland
have the lowest proportions of people who never go to
church at all, or only on special occasions. Scotland has
the highest proportion of people who never say any private prayers, followed by London and the South-East; the
North-West has the lowest. People living in metropolises
have the highest proportion of people who never go to
church, or only on special occasions; but, somewhat para-
doxically, they have the lowest proportion of those who
never say prayers or only on special occasions, and the
highest proportion of regular pray-ers.

It must be recalled that this sample is made up of people relatively recently bereaved. The widowed—those who
have lost their husband or wife—are much the most regular in private and public devotions; whereas those who
have lost their parents—particularly if they are married
themselves—worship and pray regularly somewhat less
than the average. The small group of the unmarried, divorced and separated appear somewhat more devout than
the married.

ii *The Afterlife*

The reason why the Christian clergy are so continuously involved in the disposal of the dead is that orthodox
Christianity is dogmatic that the soul continues to exist
after death, and is judged; the good go to heaven, the
imperfect (in Roman Catholic dogma) purge themselves
of their sins in purgatory, and the evil are damned to hell.
The hope and belief that one's loved ones are in bliss
are meant to be consolations to the bereaved; the fear
of damnation is meant to keep sinners in the ways of
righteousness.

By these dogmatic standards, only 11 respondents out
of the 359 hold orthodox beliefs, making some reference
to Judgment; a further 15 make references to God or
Jesus, without envisaging Judgment. A quarter of the population states firmly that they do not believe in a future
life, and the same number is uncertain; of the remainder
some 15 per cent say that they believe in a future life
but have little idea what it will be like; and the rest voice
a series of unorthodox beliefs, with no overt religious
content.

The pattern of disbelief in a future life is much the
same as that for abstention from church-going and private
prayer. It is voiced more than twice as often by men as
by women (who, however, have slightly more uncertainty); and more frequently by the young than the older,
by members of the skilled working class than by members
of the other classes (the upper middle classes having the
smallest number of unbelievers), and by people living
in the South-East and, somewhat surprisingly, in the
North-West. Those who have lost a husband or wife have
the smallest number of unbelievers, those who have lost

a parent the greatest. According to these figures a young, married, skilled working man is very likely to have no religious beliefs, a widowed upper-middle-class older woman is likely to be a practising but not orthodox Christian.

Typical of the orthodox statements are those of an 84-year-old Roman Catholic widow from the North-East, who died shortly after the survey was made:

'I believe in purgatory, that we have to suffer for a time before we go to heaven. Don't think hell can be what it is supposed to be.'

Similarly, a 75-year-old widow from the Midlands, Church of England:

'You don't go straight to heaven. There is a transmission period. There is no family life and no sex in heaven, can't imagine what it will be like.'

But the most frequent orthodox answer, usually given by Roman Catholics, is the quotation from St. Paul: 'Eye hath not seen nor ear heard, neither hath it entered into the heart of man what things God hath prepared for those who love Him.'

Typical of the other small group who feel assured of heaven and think of it in scriptural terms is a 73-year-old widow from Scotland, who describes herself as 'Christian':

'The Lord says nothing will be more glorious than to be with Him. There will be happiness and life everlasting—the Lord didn't die for nothing.'

Or a 74-year-old widow from the Midlands, Church of England:

'When we die we go to God in His glory; He paid for all our sins.'

Or a pious 65-year-old widow from Scotland, a member of the Church of Scotland:

'You go to sleep and when you waken up then it is judgment day, meet all your dear ones then.'

A 34-year-old building foreman from the South-East (13), Church of England but not a churchgoer:

'A spiritual state where I feel you will be able to see your family growing up. I don't feel any of us know much about it in fact, but I am sure that we are promised more than this life—a life after death through Christ's life where possibly you can somehow know what those still on earth are doing and see where they need help and guidance.'

This last quotation fades into the most popular concept of the afterlife held by this sample of bereaved people—watching over or rejoining one's loved ones. It is exceptional in that it does mention Christ. The 49-year-old wife of a director of a small firm in the South-East, a Methodist (14), who had recently lost her father, said:

'I don't know, but I have lost so many close relatives and I know they are able to watch over us here and give us help and guidance and I don't believe we are meant to know what it will be like until our time comes, so I am satisfied that everything does not end here—in my own mind I am sure of that.'

A 70-year-old widow from Scotland, a pious member of the Church of England (19):

'Fine—awfully bonny—you will see all the people that belonged to you. Just before my brother died he saw Mother standing at the foot of the bed.'

A 75-year-old widow from the North-West, Church of England:

'I think we become spirits and that if I see any of my family about to make a mistake I will suffer because I will be unable to prevent it.'

A 48-year-old clerical assistant from the North-East (20), Church of England:

'We shall see our dear ones again—no troubles or trials—not floating around on clouds in luxury—a working community—for needs, e.g. food and clothing.'

The 41-year-old wife of a Midlands sales manager (6), a Methodist:

'A place where there are no worries and where we meet all relatives and friends. A place where we don't worry about money.'

This consoling belief in rejoining or watching over one's loved ones is held by 17 per cent of the women, but only 3 per cent of the men, widows voicing it particularly frequently.

Among the 80 people whom I re-interviewed, 19 were positive that there was a future life, 16 were equally positive that there was not; the remainder were either unwilling to express any opinion at all, or stated in various ways that there was no possibility of knowing the answer to such a question. The minority of firm believers seemed to derive considerable comfort from their convictions. Thus, the wife of a sales-manager in the Midlands (6), quoted above, who had recently lost her father said:

'I definitely believe in a future life, yes, there's no point in living otherwise. I should imagine I'll see my father again.'

The 45-year-old widow of a shop-owner from the North-West (21):

'I'm one of those who believe that those up there can look down and see us down here. It's a comfort.'

The wife of a director of a small firm in the South-East (14), who had lost her adoptive mother:

'What I feel, if I've got any worries I used to take them to her, you see, and I feel that I should get some sign from her, somehow, that puts me on the right track . . . I still feel that if I had any worries and I prayed for help and guidance from her I would get it. . . . There *is* a life hereafter. Lots of people think this, but one thing I feel—I shall meet her again. I suppose really it's—at the back of it it is a real comfort, although I feel that she's gone now, at this moment, at the back of my mind there's still the feeling that one day we shall meet again.'

An 85-year-old widow from the South-West (22), reminiscing about her youngest boy:

'He was killed in the Air Force in the war, my youngest boy, and he often comes back and speaks to me . . . and I was laying—missing him you know—with a light over my bed—if I do say it, I'm his mother, he had a lovely face—and all the time I was thinking, I hope he's safe; and a voice said, "It's all right Mum"; and I thought, Thank God he's all right; but he'd gone. Still, I think I'll see him again some day. In fact it's kept me going.'

The elderly wife of a director in the Midlands says that she often feels when she is working round the house that her mother is still with her, and watching over her.

The second most popular view of the afterlife, after re-joining or watching over one's loved ones, is of a vaguely blissful condition; some respondents stress the positive features—beauty, rest, peace—and others the absence of worries or evil. These views are held by 15 per cent of the women and 7 per cent of the men, and are particularly popular in the upper middle and professional classes. Thus, a 40-year-old schoolmaster from the Midlands, a pious Methodist:

'I don't really know. I hope like this life, but without miseries and worries and without what we are going through now.'

A 19-year-old shop-assistant from Scotland, a non-observant member of the Church of Scotland (23):

'Much more pleasant than living—more contentment.'

The 47-year-old wife of a semi-skilled worker from the South-East, Church of England:

'Altogether different from this life—no worries, no pain and we shall be with our relatives again. Don't know what it will be like, but I know there is an after-life. I have faith in that—I know we are all here for a purpose and this life is not just the end of everything. I am not concerned really as to how exactly it will be—I am satisfied that there is another existence after death.'

The 49-year-old widow of an unskilled worker from the South-East, a pious member of the Church of England:

'I hope it will be a little better than this—we are hoping for better things—more friendly and neighbourly. People don't seem too friendly these days—they are more stand-offish.'

A 48-year-old part-time barmaid from the North-East (17), Church of England:

'You will go to a nicer world—no worries, no enemies. Everyone the same and at peace. I have visions of my husband who once said to me (in a vision); "I wish you were here, but it is perhaps too quiet for you here." It must be peaceful and quiet.'

A 63-year-old widow from the North-East, a Methodist:

'A river with flowers either side, wide and then it narrows until you cross easily.'

All the views so far quoted and illustrated are held far more by women than by men. The only concepts about the afterlife which are advanced equally by men and women are the unorthodox notions that the next life will be just like this one or, explicitly, reincarnation. These views are advanced by 9 per cent of both sexes. They of course do not correspond to the dogma of any Western Church; the relative prevalence of such ideas is still unexplained.

Typical of such notions are the following quotations. A 50-year-old tailor's cutter from the North-East (10), nominally Church of England:

'Coming back in some shape or form. You go into the land and nature sends you back in some form, don't know quite what.'

The 43-year-old wife of an accountant from the South-

East (9), an observant member of the Church of England:

> 'Sometimes I think we are reincarnated. Our afterlife is what we have left behind us in our childhood, and maybe our spirit lives in heaven.'

A 44-year-old tool-fitter from Scotland (12), a lax member of the Church of Scotland:

> 'Come back to earth as some other thing.'

A 34-year-old shoe repairer from the Midlands, nominally Church of England:

> 'You come back on this earth in a different sex.'

A 55-year-old wife of a professional man from the Midlands (18), non-observant Church of England:

> 'Come back to earth as member of a family—that is, new member of the same family, reincarnation in fact.'

A 60-year-old shopkeeper from Scotland (24), Church of Scotland:

> 'The stars we see above are people who have gone before us shining down.'

A 30-year-old bus driver from Wales, Church of England:

> 'I cannot really say, but I believe we come back to earth in another form and relive life.'

A 40-year-old wife of a lorry driver from the South-East, Church of England:

> 'I think we are reincarnated—as someone dies a baby is born.'

A 48-year-old widower from Scotland (25), a butcher, Church of Scotland:

'If you come back you will have gained experience from mistakes made in previous life.'

The 45-year-old wife of a disabled soldier in the South-West (26), a practiser of Yoga:

'Reincarnation, until you actually reach salvation, but I don't know what that will be like.'

The last two quotations could be considered fairly orthodox statements of Buddhist beliefs.

The few members of the modern sects, such as Spiritualists and Christian Scientists, are articulate and, I dare say, orthodox in their beliefs about the afterlife, presumably because membership of such sects is elected in adult life. Thus a 73-year-old widow from the North-East (27), living alone, a Christian Scientist:

'It is like a misty scene—a ship goes off into the horizon, but it never quite disappears until you go to join them.'

A 63-year-old widower from the South-West (28) with his own business, a Spiritualist:

'We believe that our body is only on loan to us in this world. The world we go to is like this one, only better, and it is always daylight—the sun always shines.'

A 63-year-old widow from the Midlands, living alone, a Spiritualist:

'Next plane to this is the astral plane where we rest until it is decided which plane we go to, all depending on how our life has been spent on this earth. We can come back to earth if we so wish in spirit form.'

I have chosen these typical quotations to demonstrate
how very small a role dogmatic Christian beliefs play in
the hopes and fears of a cross-section of British people
mourning the death of a near relative. The absence of supernatural fears is the more surprising since a quarter of
the population say that they believe in the Devil. This is
the only form of supernatural belief (of those asked
about; I thought a direct question whether the respondent believed in God would not get an honest answer)
in which the difference between men and women is not
marked; though men have a distinctly higher proportion
of disbelief, women of uncertainty. Belief in the Devil is
very slight among those under 34, among inhabitants of
the metropolises, and in the South-West; it is highest in
the North-West, with its high proportion of Roman Catholics. It would seem that the Devil who is believed in is
active in this world only; not a single respondent voiced a
belief in eternal damnation.

iii   The Clergy

For the great majority of the respondents, the clergyman who conducted the funeral was a technician hired
to do his job in much the same fashion as the undertakers
or monumental masons; a continuing relationship was no
more looked for with the former than with the latter. Of
the 80 people I interviewed, only 14 made any spontaneous mention of their clergyman or minister; and half
of these were in Scotland. In Scotland, it is customary for
members of both the Scottish and English Churches to
have a service, conducted by the clergyman or minister,
in the house of mourning for the relatives, prior to a second and more public service in the church; and when the
minister or clergyman had come to offer consolation and

help this was remembered with appreciation. An inconsolable widow of a baker, aged 53 (29), said:

'The minister was awfu' good. He and the doctor was both here. And after it was all over the minister came to see if I was all right and if I wanted a job. Of course, I go regular to the Church and the Women's Guild.'

Four other Scottish mourners spoke appreciatively of the minister's goodness and helpfulness in calling to offer consolation and assistance; two others, both men, were bitter because the minister had not called. A rather dour 71-year-old widower (30), a former worker in a jute factory, remarked:

'The minister's never been to see me since the funeral. He needn't bother to come now, because if he does come I wouldna' say owermuch.'

A 60-year-old shop-owner (24), who had lost his mother to whom he was very deeply attached, complained that he had never seen the minister since the funeral, that he thought the minister might have been able to give him the help he needed, but had not 'and that's what puts me against them.'

Just because the customary link between clergyman or minister and parishioner is closer in Scotland, and the formal ritual of mourning more completely maintained, any dereliction from what the mourner considers the minister's duty evokes resentment and hostility which is very seldom voiced in England.

When such complaints are made in England, they tend to come from the settled residential towns and villages where the role of the vicar is still generally meaningful. Thus, the widow of a retired civil servant in the South-West (31):

'I was a bit annoyed with the clergyman. We'd had a new one, he'd been here for over two years before my husband died, and he'd never been up to see him. The clergyman who was here before, who was a great friend of my husband's gave the service; he came over from [a town nearly a hundred miles away].'

The widow of a retired serviceman, also from the South-West (32), whose husband had been ailing 7 years:

'We never had no help, not from anybody, and it made me very bitter. Do you know, my husband was a good living man, he was confirmed, he was a really good living man; everybody liked him. But do you know, the vicar came and saw him once, he never saw him after. . . . Do you know, when the harvest festivals were on—my husband—nobody ever sent him a bit of fruit; and I heard one day that at a certain harvest festival, the people that was there were having the stuff. The vicar was no help, not one bit. There is a nice woman next door, she'll help. I got bad hands, you see. But after my husband died, nobody came to see me— no one, and that hurt me more than anything. When I could have done with company, I had nobody, nobody. That really got me.'

From the South-West, too, come echoes of the doctrinal disputes which rent the Church of England in the last century. A courageous and pious 85-year-old widow, living alone (22) said:

'The one thing I do miss is going to church—not being able to get out, I miss that terribly. [The present vicar does not call.] I keep in touch with my old parish, St. ——; you know I always keep in touch with them, they come and see me. In any case they're too high church round here; they burn incense, and I always think there's something *evil* in doing that.'

There is of course some appreciation, as well as some criticism. A very recently widowed woman from the Midlands (33), whose husband was cremated said:

'It was a marvellous service and a marvellous vicar. My husband's business friends were there, and the vicar stood near me and spoke to me; he was marvellous really, he read some marvellous passages to me. I'm peculiar, I believe in the New Testament.'

The widow of a colliery maintenance engineer from the North-East (34) found the vicar's visit a real consolation; and a very humble, deaf old lady from the North-West (35), who'd lost her husband after more than 50 years of marriage excused the Church of England clergyman for not visiting her:

'He came to me at graveside, minister, he said he would come and see me, but he hasn't been yet. He will be coming; it's a big parish.'

It would seem to an outsider that the English clergy are missing a major opportunity for charity in failing to visit the recently bereaved in their parishes, even if they are not churchgoers. For it must be emphasized that the majority of the people I interviewed made no spontaneous mention of the clergy at all, though nearly all were questioned about the type of religious service that had accompanied the burial or cremation, about visits and help in the days after bereavement, and the consolations (if any) they had found in their grief.

CHAPTER THREE

THE FUNERAL AND AFTER

i *Disposal of the Body*

As has already been stated, burials and cremations are almost always accompanied by religious services; only two of the respondents reported non-denominational interments. There are slight discrepancies between the denominations to which the respondents claim adherence and the type of service at the funeral of their near relative; the proportion of Church of England (and, to a lesser extent, Church of Scotland) ceremonies is greater than the number claiming adherence to those creeds, and the proportion of Nonconformist and Roman Catholic ceremonies less; the group who stated that they had no religious denomination gave their relatives the rites of the Church. On at least one occasion, the choice of rite to accompany the disposal of a body was the cause of family disagreement: a 72-year-old spinster from the North-East was in a nervous state after her brother's death because her sister-in-law had given him a Church of England funeral when he was by rights a Roman Catholic.

Nearly a quarter of the Roman Catholics reported a Church of England funeral for their near relative; there is no evidence to show whether this was due to mixed marriages or to lack of sectarian feeling; half of those who claimed adherence to no sect provided similar rites, as did a fifth of the Nonconformists. Church of England funerals are especially frequent in the upper middle classes;

their proportion increases slightly with the age of the respondents.

The general sample were not asked whether their relative had been buried or cremated; but of those whom I re-interviewed and questioned on this subject, 40 had been cremated and 27 buried. The number who had chosen cremation (there is no choice allowed for practising Roman Catholics[1] or Orthodox Jews) is rather surprisingly high—according to the Cremation Society there were 41 per cent cremations in 1963. Among these selected informants, cremation was overwhelmingly preferred in the South-West and in the North-East; in Scotland burial was preferred.

A few respondents felt deeply about the method of disposal of the body. A widowed old-age pensioner from Scotland (19) spoke for several people in claiming that cremation was contrary to the Biblical injunction 'dust to dust', and, furthermore, that bits of the 'box' are bound to get mixed up with the ashes. A 45-year-old widow from the North-West (21), whose husband had collapsed and died on the football field said:

> 'At the actual service, about half-way through it, I didn't want to cry because somehow a cremation—to me it doesn't seem as final, to me, as when you see somebody go down in the ground . . . to me the cremation service was so lovely, yet it seemed a bit unfinished as if nothing was as definite as when you see them go down in the ground.'

Similarly, a slightly older widow from the South-East (36):

> 'I'd like to be cremated. I had my mother cremated,

[1] By a papal decree of 1963, Roman Catholics were permitted, for the first time, to arrange cremations.

I think it's healthier. I think for my husband, who was buried, it was too final. A lot of people disagreed with me. I wouldn't like to be buried, that's too final.'

A number of respondents advanced aesthetic or hygienic reasons for preferring cremation; if the body had been deformed, or wasted by disease, or mutilated, it was apparently felt that it was more fitting that it should be burned. 'We thought it wiser,' said an elderly woman from the South-East (3) of her adopted daughter, her niece, who had been afflicted with acromegaly. 'Especially with the kind of disease it was,' said a widow from the Midlands (2), whose husband had died of cancer.

A second factual reason, given by a few informants, was that of economy. A widow in Scotland (11) whose husband had died of a heart attack in the South of England explained that she had chosen cremation 'on account of you see his family wanted him brought back here; I thought I would keep the expense down, doing that'. In many cases, it would appear, cremation is chosen because it is felt to get rid of the dead more completely and finally than does burial.

As far as I can tell, the question of the expense of a funeral or cremation does not seem to have borne hardly on any of the respondents, not even on those living on old-age pensions or National Assistance; the display and expense of a 'lovely funeral' seem to be completely things of the past.[2] The one item of expense which was men-

2 By common law every person who dies (with the exception of executed murderers and, until very recently, suicides) has the right to burial in the churchyard or burial ground of the parish in which he resided or, alternatively, of that in which he died. The only inevitable expenses are the published and modest fees of the incumbent who conducts the service and one of £5 or thereabouts for the sexton who digs the grave. If exclusive right to a place in the cemetery is desired, the cost will be between £5 and £50, dependent on the size and position of the site. The cost of a cremation is between 3

tioned by several of the poorer respondents was the erection of a headstone over the grave when their relative had been buried; a number were saving up, and stinting themselves, for this purpose. This expense is, of course, avoided when the body is cremated. Crematoria have halls or gardens of remembrance in which plaques can be erected; but such a plaque was only set up by one informant, out of the 40 who had had their relative cremated. Fourteen of them had had their relative's name inscribed in the Book of Remembrance, which is a feature of many crematoria. This is described as an expensive volume of vellum, with one page for every day of the year. On each day the book is opened at the appropriate date; and on this anniversary the mourners can go and read their relative's name and take flowers. The cost of an entry into such a book is stated to be between two and eight guineas.[3]

---

and 9 guineas, and the fee to the minister conducting the service between 10s. and 21s. These figures are derived from *The Disposal of the Dead* by Polson, Brittain and Marshall (especially pp. 157, 196–199, 330). This authoritative work has a section on the embalming of the dead; but, as far as I can discover, this is still an exceptional practice in Britain.

Under the National Insurance scheme, everybody who has paid at least 26 weekly stamps since July 1948 and at least 45 contributions of any class in the last completed contribution year, is entitled to a death grant of £25, which is adequate for the basic expenses. The only people not covered by this scheme are men born before July 1883 and women born before July 1888, who would have been retired before the scheme came into force. For men born between 1883 and 1893 and for women born between 1888 and 1898 the grant is £12 10s. 'because death grant was not provided under the former State insurance schemes and only national insurance contributions since 5th July 1948 count towards it'. In the case of a person under 18 at the time of death, £7 10s. is paid for children under 3 (other than stillborn babies); £13 10s. for children between 3 and 5; and £18 15s. for children between 6 and 17. 'The amount paid to a claimant may also be limited to the amount of the funeral expenses when they are less than the full rate of grant payable.'

[3] *The Disposal of the Dead*: Polson, Brittain and Marshall, edited by C. J. Polson, p. 157.

When they attend a funeral or cremation, four-fifths of the men, but less than half the women, indicate that they are mourners by their dress. The difference in practice between the sexes can no doubt be in large part accounted for by the fact that the traditional signs of male mourning—a black tie, and also often a crêpe armband—are relatively cheap and relatively inconspicuous; whereas the traditional all-black mourning outfit for women is neither. This does not, however, seem to be a full explanation; a few women (5 per cent) made minor modifications to their costume to show they were mourners (compared with two-thirds of the men); one man and two women in five wore predominantly black clothes; a fifth of the men and over half the women (52 per cent) gave no public indication that they were mourners.

This abandonment of the wearing of mourning by women does seem to represent a major change in British customs over the last 50 years; it is also a reversal of the practices of Christian Europe, where it was, and is, traditional for women to indicate their bereaved condition more markedly and for a far longer time than their male relatives.

For the minority of women who do wear mourning this persistence in its display still holds good. A third of the men, but only a tenth of the women, abandon their signs of mourning within the month; 18 per cent of the men and 22 per cent of the women wore mourning for more than three months after the funeral.

These persistent wearers of mourning, who follow the older traditions, can be identified with some precision. They are predominantly over 45, from the unskilled working classes, somewhat concentrated in the larger towns and in the North-West; and it is husbands or wives they mourn, much more frequently than any other relative. These distinctions in mourning clothing are much less marked on the day of the funeral. The South-West and Midlands show, by a small degree, the highest proportion of people who make no changes in their costume for the funeral.

For the old-fashioned and the old the omission of such signs of mourning can be very distressing. The 67-year-old widow of a colliery maintenance engineer in the North-East (34) considered that the most painful of all her memories was:

> 'It's just the son came when his father was dying, he even came to the funeral, he had a grey tie and not a black tie, and I thought how awful it was. That did affect me—it did, yes.'

The abandonment of the wearing of mourning (apart from a black tie on the day of the funeral) is considerably more advanced in the upper middle and professional classes than in the rest of the community, in the South-West and the Midlands, and in the bigger towns. Scotland has the lowest proportion of people wearing no mourning clothes. The young, under 34, are slightly more likely to wear signs of mourning on the day of the funeral than are their elders; but, with insignificant exceptions, they give up such clothes within the month. The customs of mourning dress, which were general when I was a boy, are now predominantly maintained by the old, the poor and the unskilled.

ii *Family Gatherings*

Immediately after the funeral the mourners gather in the house for a family meeting, sometimes accompanied by prayers, in three-quarters of the cases. This practice is

nearly universal in Scotland and the North; it is less frequent in the South of England. It is also somewhat more
general in the larger towns; but in general the distribution of this custom is much the same for people of all
ages, of all social classes and of all creeds. Apart from the
religious rites accompanying the disposal of the body, this
is the most widely spread ritual of mourning in Britain
today.

In the days after the funeral, there is a likelihood that
special visits will be paid by relatives and by neighbours,
those by neighbours being slightly more common. Only
in about a quarter of the cases will there be no ceremonious visits of any sort. As with the gatherings after
the funeral, these ceremonious visits of condolence are
most general in Scotland and in the North-East; they are
least frequent in the South-East and North-West; in these
latter areas the visits are more likely to be from neighbours than from relatives. Neighbours are particularly attentive to the widowed in the bigger towns. The fewest
visits of condolence are received by mourners in the
skilled working class and in the upper middle and professional classes who have lost a parent or a sibling; but
such visits are a more general custom than I had assumed;
their incidence is greater when the mourners are young.

iii Gravestones

For Roman Catholics[4] and Orthodox Jews burial of the
dead is enjoined; and for the latter so is a visit to the
cemetery on the anniversary (counted by the Jewish calendar) of the death. But for those whose creeds allow a
choice between burial and cremation, the opting for burial implies the acceptance of a style of mourning of a

4 See footnote 1, p. 38.

different nature from that implicit in cremation. It also implies a willingness to engage in continuous extra expense to keep green the memory of the dead. A gravestone is so substantial an outlay that, in at least three cases (5, 35, 37) poor mourners had to save up for over a year to make up the money; the taking of flowers and keeping the grave neat and decent are further continuous expenses.

Of the twenty-seven who had opted for burial, all but four had erected, or were saving to erect, gravestones; of these four one was an old-age pensioner on national assistance, one had quarrelled with (or been quarrelled with by) his wife's family, one had no love for his dead parents (38), and one was a Christian Scientist who denied the 'reality' of death. Of the remainder all but four visited the graves and tended them; three of these were prevented from doing so by reasons of distance or ill-health; the fourth was a practitioner of Yoga who had followed out her sister's wishes in having a stone erected for her (26), but gave no intellectual support to the practice.

All the remainder made regular visits to the graves of their dead relative. Ten of these make relatively infrequent visits, ranging from once or twice a year to once a month; the rest go so frequently that a visit to the cemetery becomes an important part of their weekly routine. This routine visiting is particularly common in Scotland; but there is no part of the country which does not have some examples. The poor widow of a Scottish baker (29) goes to the cemetery:

'When the good weather's in every fortnight. I don't take the flower, but he gets a wreath every Christmas. It's all we can do.'

A Scottish local government employee (39) visits his mother's grave every Sunday; so too does a seventeen-year-old youth from the Midlands (40), accompanying his mother to his father's grave; so also does the widow of a taxi-driver (36) from the South-East. A disconsolate widower, a cement worker, from the South-East (41) goes 'every week, sometimes twice a week; I've got flowers planted'. The wife of a jobbing gardener who had lost her mother, also from the South-East (5) and whose family was saving up for a gravestone in the distant cemetery said:

> 'One of my sisters goes twice a week; and I usually go once a fortnight—it's a bit expensive.'

The wife of an assistant sales manager in the Midlands who lost her father two years ago (6) says of her 69-year-old mother:

> 'She won't live with any of us because it's not fair to intrude on the younger folk. She's got her memories and she's quite happy. . . . At Christmas she comes to one of us. She won't stop with us because she likes her own bed; and she says she's near to my dad—he's buried down the road. The stone cost her about £50. She visits the grave twice a week and buys flowers once a week, and she can't afford it. I go on Saturday if it isn't wet . . . [after the funeral] I wasn't exactly sleeping, but lying awake; and if it was snowing I used to say "Think of our poor Dad in that churchyard." '

The proprietor of a small shop in Scotland (24), who lost his mother fifteen months ago, takes flowers to her grave regularly twice a week; and a retired stoker in the Midlands (4) visits his wife's grave—she died in 1960—every week on Sundays, Tuesdays and Thursdays.

An independent writer from the South-East (8) told of the precautions taken by his parents to avoid such a continuing cult:

'My grandfather insisted that it should only be a wooden cross, so that it would only last a lifetime and then rot. My mother was much the same, and did ask us that if we put up a memorial, it was to be a small one in Bath stone, because it weathered quickly, and after 30 years you can't see an inscription.'

By and large, the choice of cremation obviates such a cult. Quite a few informants go to the crematorium on the anniversary of the death, when the 'Book of Remembrance' is open with the name of the deceased inscribed; and three people (2, 14, 31) who had arranged cremations by the express wishes of the deceased treated the crematorium rather as if it were a cemetery. The wife of a director of a small firm in the South-East (14) explained that her uncle and aunt who had been her adopting parents:

'Were cremated; it was their wish to be cremated. They'd got no children of their own; and they said that they'd far rather know that they were in a garden of remembrance than a grave that was neglected; because the grandparents and so on who've got graves in Highgate cemetery . . . where all the young have moved away, there's just so much money sent every year to the upkeep of the graves, you see; and they felt they didn't want that.'

This woman still mourns deeply for the loss of her adopting mother, bursting into tears—in her phrase 'boiling over'—at any mention or recollection of her; she still prays to get advice from her and would, I think, have liked a grave to tend.

CHAPTER FOUR

GRIEF AND MOURNING

i *Public Signs of Mourning*

In nearly every society of the world for which mourning practices have been reported, it is customary for people bereaved of near relatives to abstain for a traditionally fixed period from some social activities and from public diversions. For a period, mourners lived in partial social seclusion, as they worked through and came to terms with their loss; the end of this period might be signified by a return to normal dress and a complete re-entry into all social activities; or, as in traditional England, the process might be a prolonged one, with gradual modifications of costume (as the move from 'deep mourning' to 'mourning' to 'half-mourning' dress), signifying the types of social life and diversions which were deemed suitable at that stage of the mourning process.

These customs have practically disappeared in England, though they are observed by over a third of the Scottish mourners. In England as a whole less than a fifth of the respondents said that they gave up any leisure activities for a time after the funeral, and in the Midlands and Western half of the country this figure falls to little more than one in ten; the vast majority hid their grief and, according to their statements, acted 'as if nothing had happened' in any situation where they could be observed.

In the minority of cases when diversions are given up, the period is usually a short one; for a week or so, mourners may give up visits to the cinema or theatre, watching TV, dancing, sports, and club activities, in that order. These abstentions are chiefly practised by the young and unmarried, in mourning for the loss of a parent, usually a mother; two typical cases of prolonged abstention from amusement after a mother's death are a 48-year-old clerical assistant from the North-East (20) who gave up dancing and going to the cinema for six months; and an unmarried 50-year-old engineer from Scotland who gave up tennis, badminton, first aid activities and Civil Defence for a year. Such abstentions occur chiefly after the death of a parent; they are much less frequent after the death of a husband or wife, and practically never occur after the death of a brother or sister. Indeed any overt abstentions after a sibling's death are most uncommon. A very few widowers give up their club activities for a little after the death of their wives.

A tiny group (less than 4 per cent) cut down on their social life for a time—visit friends less, or, in a single case, entertain less; none of these people come from the largest towns. But with the general conspiracy to pretend that death has not occurred and that nobody is grieving, two-thirds of the respondents think that bereavement meant no difference to their social life; the frequency of contacts with their friends did not change. Of the remainder, 20 per cent said that they saw more of their friends than before their bereavement, 15 per cent less.

Those who felt that their friends rallied round them in their grief came from Scotland in particular (where, according to this survey, all the rituals of mourning are more observed), followed by the South-West; people from the Midlands in comparison thought that they saw less of their friends after their bereavement. In general, friends were more attentive to mourners who were over 45, lived in the smaller towns, and particularly to the widowed. Mourners in the unskilled working classes noticed the most difference in the behaviour of their friends; 28 per cent thought they saw more of them, 18 per cent less; the corresponding figures for the skilled working class are 13 and 14 per cent. The middle and professional classes say that their contact with their friends remained steady; 17 per cent state it was more, 8 per cent less, than before their bereavement. It is above all the younger respondents and those living in the big towns who feel (in nearly a third of the cases) that they saw less of their friends after bereavement than before. Except coincidentally, this group is not the same as that which chose to abstain from social intercourse for a period; it would seem that they have been avoided, rather than that they have desired privacy or loneliness.

ii Physical Changes in Mourning

Although mourners can avoid giving any social expression to their grief, grief is none the less real, a deep, complex and long-lasting psychological process with physiological overtones and symptoms; and of these the most widespread are disturbances of sleep and loss of weight.

Two-thirds of the women mourners and two-fifths of the men stated that they slept less well after their bereavement than they did before; over half the bereaved population suffered from disturbed rest. Significantly, I think, the incidence of disturbed sleep tends to be higher in those areas where mourning is least ritualized—in the

Midlands, and in the biggest towns. In the upper middle
and professional classes disturbed sleep, or the possibility
of it, seems to be dealt with by the doctor's almost routine prescription of hypnotics (according to a number
of informants). The effect of barbiturates on people suffering from severe grief seems to have been inadequately
studied; more than one informant described an experience similar to that of a recent widow in the South-East
(36):

> 'No, I can't sleep. The hospital sent a couple of pills
> for me and, do you know, I took one and went to bed,
> and I literally shook all over. I thought they had given
> me the wrong pills and were killing me. I said, "Never
> again will I take a sleeping pill!" I literally shook for
> an hour. . . . Do you know, it was a week before I
> could go to bed without shaking.'

The prescription of such unaccustomed hypnotics is
kindly meant; but on occasion they have considerably
added to the mourner's distress.

The younger the mourner, the more likely it is that his
or her sleep will be disturbed; and it is only a minority
(17 per cent) of the widowed who consider that their
sleep was not modified by grief.

There is a tiny group (between 3 and 4 per cent) who
think their sleep improved and that they gained weight
after the death of their parent (in the majority of cases)
or other close relative. It seems likely that these few people were tending invalids whose death was not in doubt;
their release from such duties and from the accompanying apprehension might have resulted in improved health.
This cannot be determined from the tables, for the number is so small; and this small group was markedly unwilling to talk about their experiences.

Fewer people are conscious of losing weight during mourning—just on half the women and a quarter of the men did so. This change is reported more by those under 44 than those above that age, by mourners from the North-East and North-West and from the bigger towns; a very high proportion (over half) of the mourners in the clerical class report this, double the proportion from the upper middle and skilled working classes. Widows and widowers report loss of weight in more than two cases out of three; only one in eight of those who have lost a sibling make the same statement. I think it is perhaps significant that in Scotland, where the rituals of mourning are the more generally maintained, this symbolic eating oneself up with grief is not proportionately as high as in either the Midlands or the two Northern regions.

Although the involuntary physical changes of disturbed sleep and loss of weight are far more general than the voluntary temporary abstention from recreational or social activities, it is to a significant extent the same people who show both signs of mourning. Although social ritual no longer gives guidance to the behaviour of either the mourners themselves or the people who come into contact with them, the process of mourning still poses a prolonged problem of psychological adjustment for the bereaved with, in nearly half the cases, some of the same symptoms that accompany grave physical illness.[1]

iii Dreams and Visions

Thirty-one of the eighty people I interviewed recollected vivid dreams of the person they were mourning. Five people maintained that they never dreamt at all;

[1] The analogies between mourning and physical illness are developed to their utmost by Dr. G. Engel in Is Grief a Disease?

the remainder did not recall dreams of the recently dead.

Widows are much the most regular dreamers about their dead husbands; 15 out of 23 report this experience. Next come children dreaming about their dead parent; 9 out of 27 say that they do so. Three out of 9 widowers dream of their dead wife; 4 out of 15 dream of their dead brother or sister; none of the six desolate parents who had lost a grown child report this comforting experience.

For, on the whole, these dreams are comforting; only six informants report an unpleasant feeling-tone (four of these are dreams about dead parents). As an inconsolable poor widow of a Scottish baker said (29):

> 'I do dream, but I canna' keep it long enough. It just vanishes. You see him so nice, and try to keep it on when you wake. . . . He looks younger—aye, nice, nice. Last time I was dreaming he had lovely hair—I told Mrs. X he was younger lookin' than ever. Funny, isn't it?'

A 45-year-old widow from the North-West, whose husband had owned a small shop which was subsequently taken over under a compulsory purchase order (21):

> 'I dream of him occasionally. I had one very vivid dream. Actually, I was telling him all about the compensation; I suppose it was in my mind. If he'd answered me I would have taken his advice. I'm not one of these spiritualists; but it did seem so real at the time. It didn't upset me. There was a bit of a laugh in it as well.'

A 55-year-old widower from the South-East, employed in local government (42), whose wife had died five years previously:

'As a matter of fact, I still do sometimes [dream about her]. I wake up suddenly in the night and think that she's there, you know, and it isn't till I'm thoroughly awake that I realize that. . . . She is generally younger, as when we first married; that's the time when I dream of her mostly, I think. . . . I find them quite pleasant.'

The 71-year-old wife of a pensioned bricklayer from the South-East (37) talking about her loved younger sister:

'I dream about her too, she often comes to me, you know; we have a laugh and that; we're always together and working in my dreams, you see. Because we worked together sometimes on the land years ago [hop-picking] and we used to have a wonderful laugh and game out in the fields; and I can always see her in that field, you know, and the games we used to have.'

A Scottish school-teacher (7) who lost his mother a year ago:

'Occasionally I dream about her; strangely, it's mostly associated with scenes of my childhood. I'm a small boy, and she's very pale. Always very pale. I think that may be because I saw her when she was dead, and one of my thoughts was "this deathly pallor", you know. I've seen death in the war but this was new to me.'

It is worth noting that in these typical comforting dreams the dead person is envisaged as young; and on the evidence from these interviews I would consider that such dreams are signs that the broken relationship was a rich and happy one, and that the mourner is working through his or her grief without too much disturbance. The converse is not completely true; although all the dreams told to me with an unpleasant feeling-tone envisaged the lost

relative as last seen just before or just after death, some
of the comforting ones were also of the dead in his or
her last days. In these cases I think there is some evidence (which I cannot detail without hazarding my informants' anonymity) that there was a good deal of ambivalence in the broken relationship.

A pretty example of the two types of dream is given by
the wife of an assistant sales manager in the Midlands
(6), whose father had died in the cold January of 1963,
and whose mother (as recounted on p. 7) had kept his
body in the coffin in the front room, and made her daughter kiss him good night; she

'dreamt of him every night, with his white face, in
blue and white pyjamas. . . . For three months after
he died, I couldn't get him out of my mind; it was
horrible. . . . [Later she dreamt] of all the places we
went to with him when we were kids, and of all my
childhood days when he used to take us out. . . . He
seemed big in these dreams; actually he wasn't a tall
man. He was very good to us children, you know; he
took us everywhere.'

A number of the distressing dreams are founded on the
traumatic experience of seeing a dying or dead person for
the first time; the wife of a van-driver from the South-
West (43) dreamed of her sister-in-law after her death:

'Next couple of nights I could see her; every time I
closed my eyes I could see her. . . . I seen her when
she died. Oh, she was terrible! She must have suffered.'

The widow from Scotland whose husband had died of
a heart attack on a family outing (11) has nightmares
about finding him dead again; but she also has pleasanter
ones of 'just as we were; it just makes me feel as if next

day he was coming in', and she finds some consolation from the fact that 'it happened down in England—I can leave that part'.

The German-born wife of a skilled worker from the Midlands has nightmares about her dead mother:

'Well, she was in a coma, and it was the look on her face; the eyes were open and I knew she couldn't see me and I was trying to make contact with her. The nightmare was trying to talk to her and not being able to.'

A 61-year-old widow from the Midlands (44) says that when she dreams of her husband:

'That's a strange thing, when I do he's always one step ahead away from me; I never get any contact. . . . He looks just as he died.'

A similar nightmare is recounted by the 19-year-old wife of a miner in the Midlands (1) about her dead father:

'I dreamt he was running away and I wanted to catch him, it was terrible.'

An intelligent married woman from the South-East, who was quite conscious of her ambivalence towards her dead mother (45):

'dreamt a lot, either that she'd come back or been in hospital and the diagnosis was a mistake. . . . rather distressing dreams. . . . I never dreamt of her as a young woman, but then my mother was 30 when I was born, so that most of my adult life she was an older woman.'

A very depressed and distressed widow of a process worker in the South-East (46) dreamed that her husband

was in bed, one night, on top of her; he appeared as he
was in his last years.

This woman was in such a disturbed state, that I could
not decide whether she was describing a dream or an
hallucination; these are described by six informants. A
hale 85-year-old widow from the South-West (22) describes both experiences:

'I don't dream of him a lot. Sometimes now I see him
standing by me and he says, "Oh Agnes!"; then I wake
up and realize. . . . I go quite back in the past, it's
stupid of me. I remember I was sitting in that chair one
night and I was reading, and I thought I heard a rus-
tle; and I looked up and there he was in his dressing-
gown! I'm not a bit frightened of anything like that,
it's rather nice. It's stupid to be afraid; what is there to
be afraid of? My mother used to tell us when we were
little that if the live people did as little harm as the
dead, we'd be all right.'

A poor and lonely widow, aged 74, in the North-West
(35), said she doesn't dream of him much:

'I fancy I can see him on t' chair. That chair when
you come in, love. I've no one to talk to.'

A 70-year-old Scottish widow (19) said that 'When I'm
sitting here by the fire it comes into your mind, and you
see him, you know.' Similarly, a 64-year-old widow from
the South-West, whose husband had been ill at home a
long time before he died (32), said:

'The first three months, I used to forget. I used to
be making a cup of tea and take one into the front
room for him. Things like that. And how many times
have I heard that invalid bell!'

The only person who recounted a frightening experience was a small shopkeeper in the South-East (47) who had let his upstairs rooms to lodgers:

'I couldn't sleep in there after the wife died. I was upstairs after the wife died and I was watching television for the first time after she died; and all of a sudden I could see my wife as plain as anything, sitting in one of those chairs. I flew downstairs and never went in that room again. . . . It was very frightening. It's a lovely room.'

This unhappy man never dreams of his wife.

It seems not unlikely that such vivid experiences of the presence of the dead can occur in many cultures: and they can easily be elaborated into complex structures of belief.

iv Condolences

Nowhere is the absence of an accepted social ritual more noticeable than in the first contacts between a mourner and his neighbours, acquaintances or workmates after a bereavement. Should they speak of the loss, or no? Will the mourner welcome expressions of sympathy, or prefer a pretence that nothing has really happened? Will mention of the dead provoke an outburst of weeping in the mourner, which might prove contagious?

The only community in Britain, as far as I know, for whom this is not a problem is that of the Orthodox Jews. Among them, the mourner is greeted with the formula 'I wish you long life' and this demands no reply; after it has been spoken the conversation proceeds normally. But even people who have the advantage of this ritual are at a loss when dealing with people outside their community. As an antique dealer in the South-West (15) said:

'People are a little embarrassed to talk about these things, even if they feel quite sorry. One doesn't know quite what to do. Quite a well-known figure in [this town] who died about a week ago—well, his son who I know fairly well, I didn't quite know whether to go in his shop and say, "Well, I'm sorry about your father" or not. He has probably got plenty to think about, and plenty of closer friends. . . . I've found it a little bit awkward when people came in and spoke about my father, because I had to repeat the same thing over and over again, till I was tired of repeating it really. . . .'

Similarly, a recently widowed woman from the South-East (36) said of her friends and neighbours:

'They probably felt a little bit embarrassed; I'd have felt a little bit embarrassed. When I've met people before, I've thought: "Oh dear, what shall I say? Shall I look the other way?" and I think my neighbours have felt the same. . . . I think people tend to be embarrassed if you speak to them; they feel they must say something, and they don't quite know how to say it.'

Fifty-four of the mourners I interviewed held definite views about the expression of condolences. Twenty-eight of these felt that they had received comfort and support from the sympathy of their neighbours and workmates; twenty said that they had found them painful in various degrees; and six were resentful because nobody had offered them sympathy. These were all lonely people, all but one of them living in big cities; the two who came from the North-East were adherents and exponents of locally unpopular creeds—a Christian Scientist and a Roman Catholic. 'Neighbours—don't speak of them!' was the recurring refrain in their complaints.

It is difficult to discern any consistent pattern among those who said they 'found it easier' when their friends or neighbours did not express their sympathy. This sentiment is voiced slightly more frequently by men than by women; and in every case but one (a young man who had lost his father (40) the mourner was grieving for a dead member of the opposite sex—men for wives, mothers or sisters and conversely. In many cases it seems as though these mourners felt their response would be inappropriate, that they would show more or less grief than was seemly. Thus a young shop-manageress from the Midlands who had lost her father (48):

'People said they were sorry. I didn't want it. It hadn't affected me as tragically as they thought it might.'

More general is the fear of being overwhelmed by emotion which is not acceptable to themselves. A very recent widow from the Midlands (33) who finds no relief from weeping said:

'Meeting people was terrible, that's why I had to go to the doctor's; I couldn't face them at all. As long as they stop and say, "How are you?"—that's enough. . . . But my husband was a very popular man, and lots of people stopped me whom I didn't know. It made me cry. Anyway, I stopped taking a handkerchief with me, thinking I wouldn't cry if I hadn't got one.'

Similarly a working-class mother from the North-West, grieving for her son (49):

'I don't like people talking about it. . . . They kept coming like, but I didn't want to go out to meet anyone.'

Her husband explained:

> 'When she went out she was meeting them, see, and they kept sympathizing. . . . Well, I haven't been as bad, like. . . . Well, I'd rather them not mention him really, me own children doesn't mention him a lot; they know how it hurts, you see.'

It seems a fair generalization to say that most of those who rejected their friends' and neighbours' expressions of sympathy, or who were greatly disturbed by them, tended to be withdrawn characters, somewhat frightened of their own emotions. It is possibly significant (and not an artifact of the small sample) that the majority of these rejecters of sympathy come from the traditionally 'dour' Northern regions and Scotland. Only two of them are from the South.

It is equally difficult to find common sociological traits which would categorize those who found comfort from their neighbours' sympathy and condolences. There are slightly more women than men voicing this sentiment, twice as many working class as middle class, predominantly mourning their parents, husbands or wives; it is only for a minority that the loss of a brother or sister in adult life is publicly announced or deeply mourned. The loss of an adult child is (as will be developed in Chapter Six) so shattering that there is no comfort to be found, with very rare exceptions. My impression is that those people who welcomed their neighbours' sympathy were well integrated and happy in their communities and their work, and were mourning deeply, but without either ostentation or embarrassment. In short, my impression is that those who can accept sympathy in their grief are better adjusted socially and psychologically than those who cannot.

Such appreciation is usually expressed in fairly few words. Thus a widower from the South-East (47) running his own small business:

'The neighbours were a great help to me. . . . Very friendly. You see, I've been in this locality for years and years. I know them all; it's first names with me.'

A woman in a fulltime factory job in Scotland, who had recently lost her father (50) to whom, as an only daughter, she was very attached:

'Very good everybody was. I think it's better [that her workmates talked about her loss]. There's no use shuttin' yoursel' up inside, is there?'

A widow from the North-East, working as a bus-conductress (51), talking about her colleagues on the buses, when she went back to work ten days after her husband's death:

'Oh, they were very good, they understood; they had from the beginning; I mean they knew, they were very good.'

The caretaker of a block of working-class flats in the North-East who had recently lost his father to whom he was much attached (52):

'They all came up to me and said how they were sorry. . . . They all talked to me, and asked after things. . . .'

A professional man in the South-West who had lost his 15-year-old boy in a tragic accident (53):

'My employer gave me every consideration—in fact he gave me a fortnight off. The whole office staff was very, very good. They were kindness itself, by being not too obvious that they were sorry . . . but they were embarrassed in trying to offer sympathy.'

On the basis of these interviews, I am inclined to consider that the grateful acceptance of spoken condolences is the most reliable single sign that the mourner is dealing adequately with his grief.

My evidence does not allow me to make any similar generalization about condolences conveyed through the mails, either the holograph letters customary in the business and professional classes or the mourning cards frequently employed by the skilled clerical and working classes in the North and in Scotland (as described in pp. 8–9). When mourners did mention these postal condolences, they tended to stress the number received:

'Do you know I had sixty-three letters, and I'm answering every one. I think it's rather a coward's way to put a notice in the newspaper.' (36)

This statement by the widow of a self-employed taxi-driver in the South-East is typical; she certainly had found comfort in the demonstration that her husband had been so widely respected. Similarly, the widow of a colliery maintenance engineer from the North-East (34), whose husband had died of cancer nearly two years before my visit, kept the stack of mourning cards she had received in a convenient drawer and would have enjoyed showing them all to me. In those classes and regions in which letters of condolence or mourning cards are customary, the absence of such a courtesy will be frequently commented on and may lead to prolonged coldness between the bereaved and those who did not send the expected tribute. Receiving and responding to postal condolences are typically solitary activities.

When anything had been written about the deceased in the local newspapers this was always referred to with gratification.

CHAPTER FIVE

STYLES OF MOURNING

i *Introduction*

Up to the beginning of this century every society in the world, to the best of my knowledge, had explicit rules of behaviour which every mourner was meant to follow. In the smaller societies, and in those which had a Church or religion to which all the citizens belonged by definition, there was most generally a single set of rules which applied to people of every social degree; in the complex, heterogeneous industrial societies there were a number of accepted variants of the rules, dependent on creed, locality or financial or social status. These variants were socially determined; customs varying from the norm were followed because the mourner was a Quaker, or a Welshman, or an aristocrat; but, with quite insignificant exceptions, everybody knew how it would be appropriate for him or her to behave and dress when they suffered a bereavement and how to treat other mourners. People might feel that the accepted ritual was hypocritical, because it forced them to display more grief than they felt, or heartless, because it placed a taboo on the mention of the dead person or on any public signs of mourning.

I know of no evidence to show that this resentment of the social rules resulted in aberrant individual practice.

As far as my evidence goes, there are only three, relatively small, communities in Britain today whose members have rules of mourning available for them which are followed by a sizeable section of these communities. Of these, the most complete and detailed rules are those for the Orthodox Jews; these lay down in almost every particular the way mourners should behave. The Church of Scotland has a ritual which many of its members (perhaps particularly in the working classes) follow; and Roman Catholics from Ireland have, many of them, kept up the Irish practices of the wake even though the migration to Britain took place one or two generations earlier. These Irish Catholics, too, are predominantly working class and the group tends to be endogamous. The Orthodox Jews and the Catholics enjoin burial; the members of the Church of Scotland whom I interviewed had chosen burial in the proportion of two to one.

Outside these three small communities, the style of mourning in Britain is now a matter of individual choice (as is the method of disposing of the body). Recorded human societies have chosen among a gamut of possibilities, from the four days' intensive mourning among the Mohave Indians[1] of the Colorado river to the life-long withdrawal imposed on widows in classical China and Hindu India and the mummification of ancient Egypt or Peru, through all the gradations of calendrical rituals and observances. For nearly every position on this gamut an analogue can be found in contemporary British practice. This suggests, firstly, that the varied cultural practices recorded by anthropologists and historians may all have

[1] *Mohave Ethnopsychiatry and Suicide*, George Devereux.

originated because they were congruent with some influential person's temperament and predispositions before being elaborated into social rules; and, secondly, that when, as for the majority in contemporary Britain, the cultural rules are discarded, the varieties of individual temperament will develop spontaneously private behaviour corresponding to nearly the whole gamut of recorded social responses to mourning. At present, it is only the bereaved who are allowed—nay, forced—to choose the type of behaviour which they find congenial or consider appropriate; but it is, I think, possible to imagine a society where individual responses to other emotions would be similarly unpatterned.

Because the behaviour of most mourners in contemporary Britain does not follow any explicit rules, it would be possible to organize the information given me by my informants and the observations I made in a variety of ways. In the pages that follow I have described the different styles of mourning primarily on the basis of the amount of time that the bereaved person acted like a mourner, or, according to his or her statements, felt that they were inwardly mourning although there was no public display of their feelings.

ii *Denial of Mourning*

The modern sects of Spiritualism and Christian Science dogmatically deny the 'existence of death'; and consequently convinced adherents of these sects would be going against their tenets if they admitted mourning for those who have 'passed on'. A convinced, indeed fanatical, Spiritualist from the South-West, a 63-year-old widower who runs his own small business (28) said:

'Well, I was brought up in the movement. You don't countenance grief at all; it relieves you of the thought of grief. You've got the loss, but it's only the physical loss. [You don't feel sadness] because we look at it and treat it in a different way, what we call a more normal way. . . . The knowledge which I have today—and I say knowledge, it isn't a belief—the knowledge which I have today counts so much in life that it displaces fear and doubt and—as you would term it—grief, and they just become nothingness.'

The latest bereavement that this man had suffered was the loss of his brother, who had lived in the North-East. 'What,' he asked rhetorically, 'was the difference between his being in the North-East and being dead? It's just a question of communications.'

Similarly, a 73-year-old widow from the North-East (27):

'There's no death in Science. There's my *Science and Health* there. That I deeply believe; if you're a real Scientist you don't believe in death. . . . It's just like the pattern of a ship over the horizon, you know. We believe that. The ship goes over the horizon; it's still there, but we don't see it. It's just the soul departs.'

This lonely old lady had been a widow for forty years; her husband had been converted to Christian Science three years before he 'passed on' and 'the last thing he said to me was, Would I bring the two children up in Christian Science? He said there was nothing else besides.'

Her latest bereavement was the loss of a sister. She said that she did not mourn for her in any way. Since her neighbours were not Scientists she apparently had nothing to do with them. Both these informants seemed to be somewhat out of contact with reality and with their neighbourhood.

A socially much better adjusted woman was the wife of a disabled soldier in the South-West (26) who believed in Yoga. This woman had lost all her family (except her husband), her last bereavement being a brother and sister who, like her parents, had died young from circulatory troubles.

'It isn't,' she said, 'a death to frighten one; actually I would be grateful to have the same one . . . they had no suffering . . . I don't think about death a great deal; I've tried to get what to my way of thinking is a decent attitude, according to my lights, poor as they are. . . . My husband and I have been greatly influenced by Yoga, which happened to us about five years ago. We've been studying it seriously ever since. . . . Anyway, if one believes in reincarnation, I don't think one can regard death as anything but casting off an old suit. . . . I don't like the way our society treats death, the sort of darkness of mourning. . . . I do not go much for mourning, and all those outward shows don't mean much to me. But my family was very keen on having nice headstones and all that sort of thing, and I know my brother wanted one. . . . My sister, brother and mother all have a common grave in —— with a big headstone for Mother and two little ones for the others . . . my brother died two years ago; and I did go up last year to see if they had put this headstone up; otherwise I don't go. . . .'

iii *Absence of Mourning*

Besides those informants whose adherence to a creed outside the established Judeo-Christian traditions made them deny the importance of death, there was another group who claimed that they felt no grief for the bereavement they had recently undergone. Both men and women belong to this group, coming from varied social classes; but the relative who was not mourned for was in all cases either a parent or a brother or sister, never a spouse or a child past infancy.

The most general picture is of brothers or sisters who have drifted apart: 'I didn't see an awful lot of her,' as a school-caretaker in the South-East (54) said about her sister; 'You've got to accept these things . . . they don't worry me', in the words of a railway worker from the North-West (55) who had recently lost a brother; or, as a militant anti-religious retired worker in the South-East (56) said:

> 'Well, I used to run over to see the elder brother; I just miss that; and that's all there is about it. . . . I accept the loss, that's all.'

When brothers or sisters are not mourned it is usually because the relationship had lost all intensity; when parents are not mourned it is usually because the relationship was predominantly negative. A married fitter from the North-East (38) who had lost both his father and his mother (the father dying three years subsequently) said:

> 'I wasn't disturbed much . . . I'll tell you, I had a bit of a rough bringing up. It was quite a rough bringing up. When you've had one like that you don't grieve.

Not much—shall I say?—love. . . . They don't come into our life.'

The intelligent and articulate wife of a local government officer from the South-East who had lost her mother a few months earlier (45):

'Yes, her death was a relief, I suppose, with a guilty conscience. I suppose the fact that we didn't get on was that I was as pig-headed as she was. I can say that six months later . . . [the neighbours] were wonderful. I think they all knew that in some ways it was something that we could have wished for; I don't think I pretended to anybody that this was a very happy relationship . . . it was because we were so different. . . . My feelings are now much more what they should have been earlier. . . . I feel that now for once perhaps I can have my independence, be a person in my own right, instead of having to do the things I know perfectly well I don't want to do.'

The 41-year-old wife of a school-teacher in the North-East (57), both of whose parents had died within a few weeks of each other, did not mourn for them; but in her case it would seem that it was less the absence of love than her inability to mourn any more. Her first husband had been killed on the anniversary of her wedding-day; and this had been so traumatic an experience that even twenty years later, happily remarried and with three young children, she could not speak of it without tears welling up in her eyes and her florid complexion blanching. She appeared traumatized by this desolating experience, as though her wells of grief had been permanently dried.

iv *Mourning Before Death*

When someone one loves is dying of an incurable illness, either when the mourner knows this and the invalid
does not (as discussed in Chapter One) or when the
sufferer is in great pain, a great deal of mourning may
take place during this period, so that the eventual death
is felt emotionally, as well as intellectually, to be a release. Thus, the widow of a retired serviceman in the
South-West (32):

> 'Well, he was ill for seven years, but it was a shock
> in the end. He was a very sick man for seven years. . . .
> It was a relief because it hurt me to see him, it hurt
> me terrible; I used to have to go out the back or up-
> stairs, because I knew that as soon as he took these
> tablets, he was in pain. . . . I used to grieve terrible—
> my neighbour will tell you—I used to go out the back
> and cry, so he wouldn't see me. I miss him terribly,
> but he's really better off; he did suffer, and he suffered
> right to the end; in fact he had a terrible ending; he
> was in agonies. . . . My husband used to say things
> that he didn't really mean, and it used to hurt me; but
> the doctor said, "Mrs. ——, you'll have to go through
> more than that; Mr. —— is a very sick man, you'll have
> to bear it"; and from that day onward I did bear with
> it.'

A Scottish schoolmaster, talking about the death of
his mother (7):

> 'If I may speak personally about this, she had ob-
> viously been suffering and she was obviously depressed.
> She used to reminisce a great deal about her youth
> and so on and say that her happiest days were when

the family was young. I knew that morally she was sinking, I suppose that was natural. When I knew that
there was no hope for her, I did feel that honestly for
her own sake she would be better dead. The war scattered our family, and I don't think she ever quite got
over the loss of her two sons.'

A very depressed widower, a 66-year-old retired tracer
from the North-East (58) whose wife had been dying of
cancer over two years, found that her death was a release;
the worst had been that:

'I was worried all the time she was ill; and of course
I didn't know which way it was going to go, or whether
she'd get over it or not, you see.'

A 49-year-old widowed bus-conductress from the North-
East, whose husband had suffered from arthritis for
twenty years before dying suddenly from kidney disease
(51):

'I knew that would happen after all. I mean, when
you've lived with sickness for so many years as I did
with him—I mean at times it was pitiful to see him—
when this came and he went—I mean, for him it was
peace, wasn't it? I just had to make the best of it, that's
the way I looked at it. . . . To him, it was a relief, because he would have got—with his old complaint he
would have got that he wouldn't have been able to do
anything for himself; he was getting that way when he
died, you see.'

Four other informants spoke in very similar terms.

v   Hiding Grief

For about a dozen women the appropriate way to deal
with grief is to 'carry on', to 'keep busy', to act, at least in

public, as if nothing had happened. Only one man, out of all those I interviewed, used phrases anything like these, a manager of a caravan site in the South-East (59), about the death of his mother; and this was a short and rather unsatisfactory interview in the open air, as his widowed father was an invalid in the house. It seemed as though, on a deeply symbolic level (he was married and with a family) he had taken over his mother's role in tending his grief-stricken father. So, despite this one exception, I think this particular response can be described as feminine. Nine of the women were widows, three had lost their mother.

This response has several components. One is the generous wish not to make others unhappy in one's misery, particularly to protect children from the infection of grief. Frequently coupled with this is what might be described as psychological hypochondria, a belief that giving way to grief and mourning is 'morbid' and 'unhealthy', and that psychological health will best be maintained by endless trivial distraction—by continuing to be as active as possible. This aspect is most stressed by middle-class women without any gainful occupation; and though advocates of such behaviour are found in all social classes, a disproportionately high number come from the widows of professional and managerial husbands. Thus the widow of a high civil servant in the South-West (60) repeatedly made the point that the only way to cope with grief is to keep busy, to go out and see a lot of friends and so on. She 'kept her mind off things' by entertaining a good deal, preparing the food and doing all the shopping and housework. Variants on this theme are frequent; the widow of another civil servant in the South-West (31), with both her sons abroad, kept repeating:

'The only thing is to keep busy. . . . Keep busy, you've got to make a new life for yourself. . . . Well, if I can help anyone I will do, but the only secret is to keep busy. . . . Since I've come back [from a visit to a married son abroad] I've been doing bed-and-breakfast and now I've got two boys from the technical college. The only thing is to keep busy. . . . I think the only salvation is to keep busy. My husband was 70, so he'd really lived his life—still, I feel that his life was shortened by his experiences in the first war. . . . I'm afraid their experiences in that war have left their mark on that generation.'

The 45-year-old widow of a shopkeeper in the North-West (21) felt that she was carrying out the wishes of her loved husband in hiding her grief:

'He wasn't a person who would have wanted me to be miserable. Outsiders think that you should do this and do that; but he wasn't the type who would have wanted me to sit at home, never go anywhere, go into deep mourning and all the rest of it. . . . Well, I naturally went into mourning, but I went out; and then again I had the shop and I had to go into it, and that helped a lot. You put a bright face on, and people never actually brought it up—but you knew it was there all the time. He was one of these first-name people. . . . I suppose if I'd been in the house, I could very easily have broken down, I suppose it's some kind of complex we get; but with having to meet people in the shop—after a few days you get used to it. . . . Don't get into a rut; go out. My husband once said to me about a lady we know, whose husband had died five years before—he said, "Let's not sit near her, she's always moaning"; and I think I've always thought of that.

I want people to be able to speak to me, although on
your own in the house you get these feelings, don't you?
I get the feeling sometimes that I'll wake up, and it'll
have only been a dream and it will be gone; it's a queer
sensation. . . . I think when you've a family it's not
fair to them to be that way either. People don't want
to come in the house when there's that kind of an
atmosphere, do they?'

Although the phrasing naturally varies, the stress on
the therapeutic value of being busy, making work, is constant: 'You never get anywhere if you stay and brood',
said the 73-year-old widow of a serviceman in the North-
East. 'I was so busy at the time I didn't feel it,' said the
daughter of a businessman who had lost her mother (61).
'You must occupy your mind with something else,' said
the Scottish widow of a professional man (62) who had
died suddenly in Rhodesia. She also stated (with I think
considerable psychological insight); 'I find too if you've
got a temper it's much easier. I never cry, not about
things about myself; I think this self-pity is ghastly.'

The consideration for others in such behaviour is well
expressed by the wife of a director of a small firm in the
South-West (14), still deeply distressed at the death of
her adopting mother:

'I thought, there's just nothing you can do about it;
and all the worrying in the world won't make any difference. You've got not to upset yourself or make people unhappy round you. . . . Of course, when you've
got children, you see, you tell them that Nana—my
youngest boy's thirteen, or he will be in three weeks'
time—and you tell him that Nana died—she's gone—
and if you're unhappy about it, you see, instead of say-

ing it's just one of those things you've got to accept—
we're only here for a time sort of thing—you make them
unhappy; and I mean if you upset a boy of that age,
he'll cry and you're sort of sad with them all the time.
. . . Well you must sort of do that [hide your feel-
ings] for those around you; when you're on your own
and think about them, you do your mourning quietly,
alone. The same as you might do praying. You do it
alone and you do it just the same in your own room
as you can in a church.'

Tears came into this woman's eyes nearly every time
she mentioned her Nana, who had died twelve months
earlier; her mourning was prolonged, perhaps in part because she allowed it no outward show; but I think she
will get over it. With nearly all the others in this group
I had the feeling that, by denying expression to their
grief, they had reduced their lives to triviality, even
though their purposeful busy-ness warded off any overt
symptoms of depression.

vi *Time-limited Mourning*

I am using the phrase 'time-limited mourning' to designate a phased pattern of behaviour: a period of intense
grief typically characterized by weeping, loss of weight or
sleep, and withdrawal from some social activities, followed
by a return to physical homeostasis and a fuller social
life in one or more stages. Included in this concept are
the traditional rituals of mourning, whether established
by religious injunction or social custom; but I also include those mourners who describe their own behaviour
in such a phased fashion, even when they were not aware
of following any ritual.

In most psychological thinking and writing, and for most of the societies for which we have records, this is the 'normal' pattern. of mourning, and it is frequently regulated by the solar or lunar calendar. Among the mourners I interviewed it is, if one interprets what they say with generosity, still the most general pattern; twenty-five mourners, out of the eighty interviewed, can be considered to have followed such a sequence. Only with the Orthodox Jews and, to a modified extent, with the mourners in Scotland, was there an actual calendrical pattern; with the remainder the changes from one type of behaviour to another were determined by their autonomous feelings.

Time-limited mourning tends to be connected with the active practice of prayer and church-going. This is not inevitable; five of these mourners were agnostics. There is also a slighter correlation with the rite of burial and the erection and tending of a headstone; twelve of these mourners made regular visits to the cemetery. Men and women in equal numbers, and coming from all social classes, mourn in this fashion, and all relatives may be so mourned; in this group 8 were mourning their fathers, 4 their mothers, 4 their husbands, 3 their wives, 4 a brother or sister and 2 a child. As can be seen, it is the parents who are most frequently mourned in this fashion; and it may well be that the death of a parent, of a person a generation above one's own, can be accepted with more resignation and mourned with more spontaneity than the death of a loved person of one's own generation or of the generation below.

Much the most complete pattern of time-limited mourning still observed in England is that followed by the Orthodox Jews; since it is so sharply contrasted with

most contemporary practice it seems worth while out-
lining rather summarily the enjoined behaviour.[2]

Unless death occurs after sunset on Friday, in which
case the burial is postponed until the Sunday, an Orthodox Jew should be buried within twenty-four hours of
death, and, the more honoured the person, the quicker
will be the burial. While the body is in the house it
should not be left unattended; ideally, the sons or other
near relatives should keep the vigil, the body having a
candle at its head and feet; if no relatives are available,
professional watchers are called in.

The rabbi is sent for as soon as death occurs; and he
returns to the house of mourning about an hour before
the funeral is due to start. All the closest relatives of the
dead person should be gathered there, wearing some old
garment—such as a jersey—from which a piece is ritually
cut by an official of the burial group; this rent garment
should be worn continuously during the seven days of sitting *shiveh* (*shiveh* is the Hebrew for seven) of intensive
mourning. The rabbi says special prayers at the house,
mentioning the deceased by name and hoping that 'he/
she has found his/her heavenly world and is happy'. The
same prayers are used during the *shiveh* period.

After these prayers the coffin is carried out, and all the
mourners should follow on foot. If the cemetery is be-
yond ordinary walking distance, the mourners should
walk quite a way—say half a mile—before getting into
conveyances.

The body is taken into a special room, serving the same

[2] Since there was only one practising Orthodox Jew in the sample
I interviewed, and since I was ignorant of many of the rites and
practices he described, I interviewed two other practising and Orthodox Jews on this topic. I am particularly grateful to Mrs. Boyd Smith
for all the trouble she took to check details with rabbis and other
learned men.

function as a funeral chapel, at the cemetery; the mourners wait outside until it is placed in the centre of the room; then (in those groups where both sexes attend the funeral) the men stand on the left and the women on the right. Prayers and psalms are recited, and a panegyric of the dead person's virtues is declaimed by the rabbi and also frequently by a lay friend.

The coffin is then carried to the grave, followed by the mourners. All the sons and brothers of the dead person shovel some earth on to the coffin. All the relatives of the dead person then line up by the grave; and all the visitors walk down the line of mourners, shake them by the hand, and say in English, 'I wish you long life'. This phrase is only used in this context; it is also written in letters of condolence by people who have not been present at the funeral. After the burial the special prayer for the dead, *kaddish*, is recited for the first time by the sons and brothers of the dead person.

The funeral party then returns to the house where the death has occurred (or occasionally to the house of a near relative). The closest relatives of the dead person sit on special low mourning stools (these can be borrowed from the synagogue) wearing their rent garment and special slippers without any leather in them. For the whole seven-day period the mourners should sit, thus dressed, on the low stools, unwashed and unshaven and the women without make-up, from sunrise to sunset. They should move as little as possible and do no work at all.

On the return from the cemetery a meal is provided of eggs, salt-herrings and circular rolls, beigel.[3] The

[3] According to Zborowski and Herzog, *Life is with People*, 'roundness symbolizes mourning'; and so such foods as peas or lentils are also suitable.

mourners should not feed themselves; it is a good deed to feed the mourners. After this ceremonial meal the visitors go home.

During the seven days of intensive mourning, prayers for the dead are said every morning by the men, every evening by the men and women, and at any other time during the day when ten males over the age of 13 are gathered in the room to compose a *minyan*. The mourners are meant to do nothing and in theory only to eat the food that the visitors bring them; but today in England it appears that this food is sometimes symbolized by sweets or cigarettes. ('I don't smoke and I don't eat sweets', the business-man from the North-East (63) added parenthetically when describing the gifts he was brought when mourning his first wife.) The visitors greet the mourners who either do not reply at all, or only very briefly. They then start talking to each mourner about the person they have lost.

'It is amazing,' said the wife of a business-man from the South-East, remembering the mourning for her mother,

> 'It is amazing how these visits comfort you. They talk to you and start discussing the person you have lost; picture albums are brought out and everyone reminds you of little episodes in their lives. Suddenly one laughs and enjoys those memories. One's grief is lightened; it is a most healing and comforting week. Brothers and sisters who have drifted apart come together again and recall good memories. It is a comfort.'

The man from the North-East (63) spoke in much the same way:

> 'Well, you do these things, you don't worry about them. . . . It's actually a good thing; the week of grief

gives you time to get over all the worry and what not.
. . . Even though it seems outlandish at the time—it
really is a help—you're away for a week and get over all
your grief. You get it all concentrated in one week.
. . . I always thought before [his first wife died] it was
a waste of time; but you realize when you go through
it that it isn't really; it's there for a purpose.'

The ritual enjoined for women ends with this seven-
day period; men should not cut their hair or shave for
thirty days; and for eleven months the sons or other
mourners should go twice daily to the synagogue to say
kaddish. At the end of these eleven months the gravestone
is erected and the period of mourning is over; but four
times a year prayers for the dead are said at the synagogue, which should be repeated meticulously, since 'the
souls of the dead are said to be nearest the earth', and at
every anniversary of the death (counting by the Jewish
calendar) the grave should be visited and prayers recited
in which the names of all surviving relatives and descendants are mentioned and memorial lights should be lit
in the home.

All the informants agree that they found this very concentrated and overt mourning therapeutic; the fact that
they could hide neither their grief nor their mourning
made it easier for them.

As far as my knowledge goes, there is no Christian
practice which regulates the behaviour of the mourners
to anything like the same extent. The nearest analogue
would seem to be the ritual of the Church of Scotland,
and of the other Christian sects, such as 'the English
Church' (rather than 'the Church of England') which
have adapted their ritual to that observed by the majority
in Scotland.

With this ritual it is customary for the body of the dead person to be brought to his or her home, if death has occurred in hospital or abroad, and for at least an intermittent vigil to be kept in the days preceding the funeral. On the day of the funeral the near relatives gather at the house and the minister or vicar conducts a short service for the family in the house; the funeral procession then proceeds to the church at which a second service is held, attended not only by the family but by those neighbours, friends and associates who wish to pay their last respects. After the burial those who have attended the funeral are entertained, typically at the house, with tea and sandwiches or the like; but if the family is relatively prosperous and if mourners have gathered from a distance, it is customary to give a slap-up high tea with drinks to the funeral party at a hotel.

Although this ritual does not prescribe the proper behaviour for mourners in either the detail or the duration that Orthodox Jewry does, the first days of bereavement are fairly fully occupied. Many of the Scottish mourners wear black or dark clothes for some weeks, and abstain from unnecessary social activities. Neighbours proffer help.

It is not easy to illustrate the way in which this customary behaviour makes mourning easier to work through. It was indicated by short phrases of appreciation of the help from the minister and the neighbours:

'Very good, everybody was' (50): 'I got help from the clergy—he was very nice . . . och, it's not so bad now, it was at first. I'm getting used to it now.' (19)

'One neighbour says I can just drop in any time; she makes me a cup of tea; we have a chat and then I carry on. . . . The girl [her 11-year-old daughter] was doing a paper round and I got up and went with her; it's made a big difference to me. It started me off going out and about again' (11).

'For a few days I wore mourning, which seems to have gone out of fashion a bit. . . . I felt the strain and I was in tears some of the time. I used often to cry in private, quite, quite copiously. My father did too, just before the funeral; he just dissolved. Once you have cried you do feel better.'

This last quotation is from a schoolmaster who had lost his mother (7).

The ability to weep freely, and admit one has done so, seems to be a reliable sign that mourning is being worked through and overcome. 'Oh, I did cry; I couldn't stop. . . . When you cry you get it off your chest,' said the 32-year-old caretaker of a block of flats in the North-East (52), talking about the death of his widowed father to whom he had been devoted. Before his father had died, 'of a night-time, he'd come round or I'd be at the club with him', and he still misses him sorely. For six or seven weeks he wore mourning and gave up all social activities; he was grateful to the people who came up to him 'and said how they were sorry'. With no apparent guidance from religious ritual (he was nominally Church of England) or local custom he had evolved a satisfactory time-limited ritual of mourning.

The general consensus of people who have evolved their own time-limited mourning without the guidance of ritual is that the period of intense grief is somewhere between six and twelve weeks:

'The grief never quite goes, I should think that after about three months I got over the worst of it. I knew I was on my own and I'd got to make the best of it.'

These are the fairly typical words of a 55-year-old widower in local government in the South-East (42) whose dearly loved wife had died of tuberculosis five years earlier. He wore a black armband, black tie and dark suit during that period. His wife was cremated:

'I mean, I think once the body is cremated or buried, I think that's the finish as far as the body goes. I mean, I think you can preserve their memory more at home than where they're actually buried. I'll tell you one thing I always do—perhaps it's silly, but I always buy her a little present at Christmas of some azaleas or flowers of some description; I feel that she's still in the house, you see.'

A similar ritual was observed by a solitary woman from the Midlands (44) who had lost her husband nine years ago, and her spastic son, to whom her life was devoted, quite recently.

'I'm not a coward, but I'm not one to keep going to the cemetery—I believe in helping the living. On birthdays, I put a bunch of flowers by their photograph. I can see that, you see. . . . After it happened [the agonized death of her son] I didn't want to live, I didn't take an interest in people; but my husband left me a legacy of friendship. . . . I like people; I've just come from a club now; you must get amongst people. You lose friends if you've got a long face. For three years, I couldn't bear the thought of going where we used to live, but now I can face it. Time heals.'

vii *Unlimited Mourning: 'Never Get Over'*

The comforting belief that time heals is rejected in so many words by a sizeable group of mourners (15 out of

80); the phrase used is 'never get over it', and it is employed both to describe one's own feelings and those of
others.[4] All the informants who used this phrase were
working class (two owned one-man shops); all but two
were over 50 (and these two were referring to their surviving parent); and I felt that the statement was frequently made with some complacency. I do not mean by
this that the dead person was not sincerely loved and
mourned, but rather that, within this predominantly unskilled or semi-skilled working-class group, the statement
that one will never get over it is a demonstration of how
dutiful and loving the mourner is.

The same phrase is used continuously. 'I've never got
over it. . . . You never forget,' said the Scottish widow of
a factory-worker who'd died of a heart attack (64). 'She's
never got over it—definitely not. Christmas, birthdays,
you know . . .'; a young storeman from the Midlands
(40), talking about his mother, widowed four years ago.
'I think it's a thing you never get over,' said the 53-year-
old Scottish widow of a baker (29); she added, when I
said goodbye, 'I've got a braw house with four bedrooms
upstairs; but the main thing is missing.' 'I just sit around
and mope really; . . . some people may have more guts
than me and get over it easier,' said a widower from the
South-East (47) who runs a small shop. 'It's a blow yet
. . . there are things you never get over': an elderly
woman from the North-West, talking about the death
of her younger son (49). 'It was our eldest sister, and
naturally you don't get used to it for a long time. . . .
It's a thing we'll never forget because it's one of our own,'
a van-driver from the South-West (43) said about his

[4] Peter Marris in *Widows and Their Families* reports the frequent
use of the same phrase by the working-class widows in East London
whom he interviewed; see e.g. p. 22.

unmarried sister, who, from other remarks made, seems to have been rather a burden while she was alive. 'Oh, they'll never get over it', said the wife of a retired brick-layer from the South-East (37) about her dead sister's family:

> 'No, I don't think they'll ever get over it; because each time I meet them they talk to me and that when they come up; they always bring her name up and they say, "Aunt Mary, what a shame Mother went!" . . . [The woman's husband] will never get over it. Still works, but he's awful bad hisself now. Never had a day's illness. Don't go out, he sits and watches tele-vision. . . . It was a very bad loss to me, I felt it very bad when she went. . . .'

Although these people's grief was genuine I did not feel, when talking to them, that they were in despair, as are the mourners to be described subsequently. Psychologi-cally they had, most of them at any rate, got over their intense grief; by saying they would never get over it, they were proclaiming their continued affection for the person who had died.

viii *Unlimited Mourning: Mummification*

I am using the term 'mummification' in a metaphorical fashion. The ancient Egyptians preserved their dead from the natural processes of decay by embalming the body; the type of mourner whom I wish to describe pre-serves the grief for the lost husband or wife by keeping the house and every object in it precisely as he or she had left it, as though it were a shrine which would at any moment be reanimated.

The most notorious exemplar of mummification in

recent English history is Queen Victoria, who not only preserved every object as Prince Albert had arranged them, but continued the daily ritual of having his clothes laid out and his shaving water brought. None of my informants went to quite that length; but two of them (4, 42) bought flowers at Christmas and on her birthday for their wives, dead four and five years respectively.

Four widowers and two widows treated their houses in this fashion. Everything is just as he or she left it. The visual impression is striking; the woman living in a house alone, with a man's belongings all over the room:

> 'The house is just as it was, even this; he always kept it there and the dog used to get it to go out for a walk at night; his pipe is still over there, his glasses and his hearing aid, and his tobacco. My brother-in-law wanted me to clear all his clothes out, but I couldn't—not yet anyway.' (36)

This woman was a very recent widow; another widow in the North-East (34) had kept everything in the same place for two years. A widower in the Midlands, a retired stoker, (4) whose wife had died four years previously, had her clothes all over his sitting-room; her grave was just round the corner and he visited it every Tuesday, Thursday and Sunday. A 61-year-old manufacturer in the North-West (65) had kept his large house with 'everything just as it was' for four years; he seemed to be trying to kill himself with overwork: 'I was working till half-past two this morning, and three o'clock yesterday.' A 58-year-old cement worker from the South-East (41) who was widowed fifteen months previously, worked on night-shift and spent his days keeping his house in spotless condition; the front parlour could easily have been in an 'ideal home' exhibition:

'She had her certain places for different things and I haven't shifted them at all. Everything is in the same place where she left it. . . . Of course it's a woman's job, but I'm not afraid to try. It's a full day's work altogether to do everything; I may wash one or two things myself, a few hankies, you can do small things yourself. . . . Things run just the same as she was here; the neighbours and that, they come along and everything seems, well as a matter of fact, normal. It's just that it's my feeling that everything seems empty. When you walk in the room and there's nobody there, that's the worst part of it. . . . I know when the wife died it used to take me about a day to dust round, where a woman goes around in about half an hour and makes nothing of it. . . . We [his unmarried son] share the chores between us. I sweep and dust and that in the afternoon. . . . I'm not ashamed for anyone to come in, you see. I just carry on.'

The discovery of these domestic shrines, of the material preservation of every trace of the dead spouse, was the most unforeseen aspect of the interviews I conducted; but when I mentioned this to some of my other informants, they frequently produced other examples from their knowledge. Thus, the courageous widow of a civil servant in the South-West (31) said:

'A woman two or three doors down, that's exactly what she's done. Just as if her husband's still there, and it's a year ago this week. She goes about like death warmed up. We've tried to get her out and to go about, she just won't go.'

ix   Unlimited Mourning: Despair

Since I did not interview this lady, I cannot tell whether I should have classified her type of mourning as mummification or as despair. It sounds more like despair—a term I have chosen in preference to the psychological terms 'depression' or 'melancholia'. All three terms are probably synonyms, but I consider that depression or melancholia should be reserved for psychiatric diagnoses. Despair is almost palpable to the lay interviewer: the toneless voice, the flaccid face muscles, the halting speech in short sentences. Three out of the nine mourners whom I consider to be in despair were sitting alone in the dark. Three of these mourners were widows, two were widowers, two were men in middle age who had lost their mothers, and one widower and one married woman had lost a son in young adulthood. One widow hanged herself between being interviewed in May and my attempting to see her in the North-East in November.

Only two out of these nine people had engaged in any formal mourning; these were a pious Roman Catholic (66), an old-age pensioner mourning his boy killed in a motoring accident, who found some meaning and pattern in his life from the practice of his religion; and an observant member of the Church of Scotland (24), a 60-year-old man with a little shop who was 'exceptional close' to his mother until she died fifteen months ago; he takes flowers to her grave twice a week. These two were the only mourners in despair who had had the person they mourned buried (the old-age pensioner was on National Assistance and regretted he could not erect a headstone); the other seven had arranged cremations, and, save for two inscriptions in the memorial book and one seat in a distant crematorium, had not given any formal or ritual elaboration to the disposal of the body.

It is difficult to illustrate despair from the interviews, for one of the signs of despair is the grudging speech, the monosyllables or incomplete sentences, the long silences. The 54-year-old widow of a process worker in the South-East (46) spoke about 200 words in twenty minutes; the first thing she said when she opened the door was, 'I miss him. I'll never get over it'; the last thing, twenty minutes later, 'I don't think time ever heals.' She cannot bear to be alone in the house; when her daughter, a young woman, is out of the house, she has to go out somewhere, to see her sister or to the shops. Apart from this protection, 'there's nothing I really want from anybody. I miss his company terrible.' She was full of nervous twitches.

A 66-year-old widower, a tracer, from the North-East (58), who looked undernourished, said he didn't bother to do any cooking—'anything will do for me.' His neighbours and relatives try to help him:

> 'They asked if there was anything they could do, you see, so I told them that . . . I managed all right . . . there's people tell me there's people a lot worse off than me, but that doesn't make my case better. I know it's unfortunate, but I suppose we have to face this sort of thing.'

A manufacturer in the North-West (65), whose wife had died four years earlier, was trying to kill himself with overwork. He could not bear to talk about the early days of his bereavement. 'It brings it all back, you see. . . . It's all right working, but when they go, you're down at the bottom again.' I interviewed this man two days after President Kennedy's assassination, and he remarked as I was saying goodbye:

'I'm thinking about the Kennedy family and the kiddies. I don't know. You don't think of these things till you've had a packet yourself.'

This was the longest consecutive sentence he uttered, and the only time his thought was diverted for a moment from his own misery.

None of these people in despair were very recently bereaved; at least twelve months had passed since the death of the person they mourned so insistently; their unhappiness was of a quite different nature to the intense grief which so many of the time-limited mourners reported in the first three months of bereavement. They were nearly all solitary, as it seemed by choice for (with the exception of the friendless old-age pensioner who had lost his son) those who lived alone had children or other kinfolk who were willing to share a house with them. As the wife of a sales-manager in the Midlands (6) said about her widowed mother:

'She won't live with any of us, because it's not fair to intrude on the younger folk. . . . She never bothers to get herself any meals unless you go. When we go she lays the table and gives us a damn good meal; but she never has a dinner if she's by herself. . . . The neighbours have asked her to join the Darby and Joan club; but she won't join any, she won't mix. She says, "I'm all right with my memories. . . ."'

The number of people in despair—9 out of 80—was a surprise to me. I am inclined to see a connection between this inability to get over grief and the absence of any ritual either individual or social, lay or religious, to guide them and the people they came in contact with.

CHAPTER SIX

TYPES OF BEREAVEMENT

i Introduction

Every death entails some changes in the social position and the status of the surviving kinsmen; some of these changes are slight, such as, in the majority of cases, those resulting from the death of a brother or sister; some are so profound that most languages have special words for the orphan, the child who has lost one or both parents, or the widow, the wife who has lost her husband, to indicate their special status. Since there seem to be some regularities, in Britain, concerning this change of status, the information given me by my informants is analysed in this chapter according to the relationship of the dead person to the survivor.

ii Death of Father

For fifteen of the people I interviewed—eight men and seven women—the loss of their father was the most recent bereavement they had suffered. In four of the cases the mother and father had died within a few weeks of one another; in two cases the father was the surviving parent, the mother having died several years previously; in the remaining nine cases the mother survived her husband.

On the basis of these interviews, I should consider that the survival of the mother is crucial in determining the status of the child after the father's death. When both parents died within a few weeks of one another, the change of status seems to be slight; the pattern of holidays, especially Christmas, is liable to change, with fewer or no gatherings of brothers and sisters and their children; but the survivors do not seem to consider their position altered, nor was their grief intense. The death of the parents seemed to be 'natural', in the proper order of things; none of my informants inherited any considerable property or a title. The two men who lost their widowed father were much more distressed; in both cases father and adult son had been good friends, spending much of their masculine leisure together. 'Oh, I do miss him! Of a night-time he'd come round or I'd be at the club with him. We always did that,' said the caretaker of a block of flats in the North-East (52). He had a headstone erected for his father, and visits it regularly with his children. He seems to have acted as the centre of his family ever since he married, his father and his married brother coming to him for Christmas; he mourned for six or seven weeks; but his status had not changed significantly.

The miner from the Midlands (67) felt that the death of his widowed father had removed the bond which held the family together.

> 'We always used to go down Christmas Day to see him, and there'd be one or two of the brothers and sisters there. . . . Nothing like that now.'

All the family were miners:

> 'Dad worked at the pit—"This is my son" business.

. . . When they told me about him on the Sunday I
could have dropped through the flipping floor. . . . He
just collapsed, he collapsed and died in the bathroom.
. . . It was merciful in a way; that's how he would have
wished to have gone, when his time come like . . . he
didn't suffer.'

When the mother survives her husband, her children
always seem to feel an extra burden of responsibility,
irrespective of age or sex; the widowing of one's mother
imposes a sudden and heavy burden of responsibility on
the unmarried; the responsibility of the married shifts
from their own generation and that of their children to
the generation above, the generation from whom they
had been used to receive protection and advice and whom
they now have to succour. In most cases there is also a
financial responsibility, for, as will be developed at greater
length subsequently, it is very uncommon in Britain for
a widow not to be considerably impoverished by her husband's death. The only informant who expressed no feeling of responsibility for his father's relic was the antique
dealer from the South-West (15); in this case the widow
was his stepmother, his real mother's younger sister, who
was apparently left comfortably off; this man still misses
his father, from whom he had inherited the business:

'I found that there was somebody I wanted to
speak to about certain things, you know, particularly
about the business, and it seemed a complete absence
of anybody, you know. . . .'

The wife of an assistant sales manager in the Midlands,
(6) who was very attached to her dead father, spoke for
nearly all her fellow-bereaved when she said: 'I was upset
about my father, but more about my poor mother.' This

woman has made a cult of her husband's grave, and will not sleep in the house of any of her children, so as to be 'near my dad, he's buried down the road.' The children have established a sort of informal rota for visiting her because:

> 'She never bothers to get herself any meals unless you go. When we go, she lays the table and gives us a damn good meal; but she never has a dinner if she's by herself.'

The young wife of a driver-salesman in the Midlands explained how she and her married brothers and sisters took it in turns to loan one of her mother's seven grandchildren to live with her: 'This keeps her interested. She has one of the boys with her now because she is inclined to mope in private.' In a rather similar way, a 47-year-old Scottish flax and canvas weaver (50) who was very attached to her father—she was the only daughter—explained:

> 'Well, I work you see, and she helps to keep the house. She makes the dinner and the beds and that. That keeps her mind occupied, you see. I help her in the money . . . she's not a poor widow but she's not wealthy. . . . At times you didn't know just what you were going to do, but I had my work and my family and mother to help . . . she's kept busy just now, she has her own home, you see.'

The compromise of these last two examples, whereby the widowed mother has a role in her married children's lives but maintains her own home, seems to be the best available under the current British value system, which holds that it is distasteful, almost immoral, for three generations to occupy the same house, for a widowed parent to live with her married children (this will be further discussed subsequently); in many other societies a resident grandmother is considered to be of the greatest help. The only example of this which I saw (1) was not a happy one. The middle-aged widow of a man who had died of cancer had come to live permanently with her 19-year-old daughter who was married to a miner, because:

'I was three months a widow before I came down here; it was lonely, horrible. I gave up my home . . . I'm getting used to the idea now. . . . Your life's gone, as if there's nothing left in life at all. . . . I dread Christmas coming.'

'So do I,' said her daughter emphatically; her own life—she had a baby daughter—seemed absorbed in tending to so much misery. 'We used to go out for a drink, my husband and I, but we stopped that.'

The responsibility seems to bear even more heavily on the children if they were unmarried, particularly if they are only children. The 23-year-old manageress of a shop in the Midlands (48) had been engaged when her father died three years earlier, and 'I'd been putting it off and putting it off' because she felt 'unfortunately' responsible for her mother. 'You've got to take things on yourself.' Now the story is coming to a happier conclusion. Her mother has taken a job and 'my mother's friends were quite helpful; they took her out of herself more or less. I could have done, but they were her own age group.' Now the date of the wedding is fixed and her mother 'is trying to get a smaller house; she'd rather be independent. . . . I think *now* she's glad I'm getting married, because before she thought, if anything happened to her, what would I do?'

Even more poignant is the case of a 17-year-old youth

in the Midlands (40) whose father had died of a heart
attack just before the boy was 15. He is an only son. He
took half-days off from school to look after his mother
and left school when he was 15 to take a well-paid but
dead-end job as a storeman.

> 'I was going to sit for the G.C.E.; but I felt it was too
> much. I left and got a good job; I wanted a car. . . .
> I'd lost all interest. It's only now that I realize that I'd
> have had a bit of a future. . . . It's a thing that hap-
> pens.'

He had been a notable schoolboy athlete and had represented his county abroad, but he had abandoned all
that to look after his mother:

> 'I'm the only one. I look after her, yes. . . . We live,
> I should imagine the same as a man and wife. We share
> each other's problems, and all the rest. . . . I'm go-
> ing to get married in the near future. . . . She [his
> mother] doesn't really associate with people though. If
> we go out, you see, with the girl-friend, we have a lot
> of freedom and that, but—— she's welcome and we
> have a good time, but, well, it's just one of those
> things.'

It was of course planned for the girl-friend to move in
with the young man and his mother when they did get
married. He would not contemplate his mother moving
away: 'We're happier as we are.'

In a rather similar way a 17-year-old apprentice fitter
in Scotland (64) was the sole emotional and financial
support of his widowed mother, though, as an apprentice,
he hasn't got much pay; they just manage. The widow of
a professional man who had died in Rhodesia (62) when
her elder son was 12, said:

'S. has been a terrific strength. Without him I would have gone under. I may have put too much on him, but he's that sort of type. . . .'

iii Death of Mother

Owing to women's greater longevity and the fact that, particularly one or more generations ago, a husband tended to be older than his wife, the death of a mother comparatively rarely leaves a widower father as a responsibility to the surviving children. Apart from the four cases, referred to above, in which the death of both parents was nearly simultaneous, five of the people I interviewed had a father surviving his wife's death, whereas in eight cases the mother had been a widow.

In four out of the five cases, it was a son who took responsibility for his widowed father, to a greater or lesser degree. The manager of a caravan site in the South-East (59) had his father living with him and his wife; he had given up the family home. Similarly, an unmarried 51-year-old Local Government official in Scotland (39) had his invalid father living with him and his unmarried brother. They were, he said, a very united family; either the widowed father, one of the brothers, or his married sister visited his mother's grave every day. A girl from Australia (61) whose mother had died from cancer at the age of 53, reported that her father was managing very well. 'He has a lot of friends and he's very adaptable. He cooks for himself and my younger brother lives there with him.' Every effort was made by this family to act as if nothing had happened. The cement worker from the South-East (41) who was keeping his house as a shrine to his wife (see pp. 86–87) was helped in this task by his unmarried son: 'We share the chores between us . . . you see we're doing a bit of decorating.' This son seemed to have no life of his own, no friends of either sex as far as his father knew; he was an only child.

The Scottish schoolmaster (7) felt that with his mother's death 'the centre of the home' had gone. 'There's now no focal point where we can meet.' His father had spent the last Christmas (the first since his wife had died) with him; but otherwise he didn't feel him a responsibility.

> 'Actually, he's taken up with a man in similar circumstances, whose wife died too, and they're now firm friends. Previously these two gentlemen had not seen eye to eye, but now they're firm friends.'

This pattern of friendship between two men or women widowed at about the same time is, as will be seen, a not uncommon solution for the loneliness of widowhood.

The only instance that I heard of a child having to assume the responsibilities of a dead mother in a fashion analogous to those recounted above for a dead father was that of the niece of a retired bricklayer in the South-East (37). This is a very traditional mother-centred working-class family; and the mother had died at the comparatively early age of 61. My informant was the oldest sister, eleven years older than she who had died; and for her own children, as well as for her nephews and nieces, she was still the principal person to consult and to visit. But her sister had left not only a husband, but also two unmarried sons, aged 29 and 25; and the eldest daughter kept house for them:

> 'She's got to, you see; because there's two sons going to work and the father—well you see she's got to stop at home to see to them, else they wouldn't have no hot food nor nothing.'

This girl had also taken her mother's place as what might be termed the communication centre of the family; she gathered all the news by telephone, letters and meetings and passed it on; and she entertained all the large extended family at Christmas and similar festivities. Her aunt commended her as 'a nice girl, a nice living girl, nice respectable girl' and, like the rest of the family, 'they all take after their mother—very clean, plenty of good food, nice girls, have a nice table.' The aunt realized that this girl was sacrificing herself to look after her father and brothers and thought that she would never get married.

'She had a young man, but he went abroad, salesman he was. She used to say to me, "I don't think I want him, Aunt Mary"; and I said, "Well you have your choice; you don't want him, you don't have him"; that's what I used to tell her.'

In this typically mother-centred working-class family the father's kin count for very little. 'They don't have much to do with one another,' my informant said. 'There ain't many of them here now . . . there's only about one sister, I think.' In such families the death of a mother is not only a cause for grief, but modifies the status of the survivors to a greater extent that any other death in the family would appear to do.

The wife of a jobbing gardener in the South-East (5) felt that the centre of the family had disappeared with her mother's death:

'Well, it's surprising; we girls just cling together and the boys—we don't see much of them. It's surprising— we used to see them when we had to go and see Mother; but now——'

This woman kept her mother's memory green by constant visits to the cemetery, by large photographs of her on the wall, and by constantly talking about her. She has six children of her own, including a married daughter to whom she was lending two rooms until she got a house of her own; but she still misses her mother's guidance and advice.

This lack was felt even more poignantly by the wife of a director of a small firm in the South-East (14):

> 'If I'd got worries I used to take them to her, you see; and I feel that I should get some sign from her somehow that puts me on the right track. . . . I still feel that if I had any worries and I prayed for help and guidance from her, I would get it.'

In this case it was not for her biological mother that she was mourning (she was still alive), but for her adopting mother, her aunt, who had raised her from a baby. Even twelve months after her death, she could not speak about her without tears welling up in her eyes; 'boiling over' was the phrase she used.

This was the only middle-class woman I interviewed whose grief for her mother's death was unalloyed; the usual phrase, with considerable undertones of ambivalence, is that the death was 'a merciful release'.

For middle-class men, on the other hand, the mother's death is a source of grief which often surprises them. 'I certainly didn't realize how much emotionally I relied on my mother,' said a 36-year-old free-lance writer from the South-East (8). He wept a lot at her death:

> 'I also found that I didn't mind doing it; there's nothing to be ashamed of in grief for one's mother. It was immediate and unexpected. . . . As far as her

death goes, I think we tend to look after each other more, we look after our unmarried sister, in a way that wasn't necessary when she was alive. . . . It was a severe grief, I believe it is for every man. I think it may well be more severe for a man than for a girl. They feel their father's death more.'

The Scottish school-teacher (7) said:

'Well, I just couldn't believe it. But I'm a very busy man and I must say, you know, that at times I think about her. It's a most peculiar experience; I go for several weeks and then I just think about her. Occasionally I dream about her. . . . I felt the strain and I was in tears some of the time. . . . I used often to cry in private, quite quite copiously. . . . Once you have cried you do feel better.'

This man had named his baby daughter after his dead mother.

The married proprietor of a small shop in Scotland (24) was still grieving deeply for his mother fifteen months after her death; he and his mother had been 'exceptional close' and he would still like to have her advice. He takes flowers twice weekly to her grave: 'Och, aye; it's a loss all right.' The old lady must have been over 80, for he is 60 years old.

iv *Death of Husband*

As the previous section has indicated, widowhood is the likely lot of every British married woman, for women are longer-lived than men and, usually, younger than their husbands; but although these biological and social facts are well established, no preparation, social, economical, or emotional is generally made for this eventuality. As Professor Titmuss has pointed out,[1] our retirement and pension laws are based on the assumptions that women are biologically weaker than men, since their retirement age is five years earlier, and their physical needs less, since their pension is smaller. Although many firms and some public services pay adequate retirement pensions to their employees, it is rare for these pensions to be continued undiminished for their widows; and so widowhood is typically a time of poverty, perhaps most markedly (by contrast) for women of the middle and professional classes who have grown accustomed to a comparatively large income; in none of the cases of the formerly prosperous women I interviewed had their husband 'carried' sufficient life-insurance (as their American counterparts would almost certainly have done) to maintain them in comfort, or, indeed, preserve them from want (31, 60, 62).

It is also, and this is perhaps the most recurrent theme, a period of loneliness. There is no place in the British social scene designed for widows. We have decided—and the widows have taken the decision to heart, with very few exceptions—that it is undesirable, almost immoral, for a woman to share a house with her married children; we have failed to develop any institution analogous to the Belgian *béguinages*, the lay equivalent of convents where widows can live together in comfort, and use their energies in social work. As a consequence, Britain is full of houses and flats occupied by solitary old women, often under considerable financial stress; they have literally nowhere else to go, except the old people's homes, if there be a vacancy; and for women in their 70's or 80's today these homes carry much of the stigma of the Victorian workhouse; indeed they often occupy the same buildings.

[1] Richard M. Titmuss, *Essays on 'The Welfare State'*.

The position of women left with dependent children is particularly onerous, as Peter Marris and Margaret Wynn[2] have pointed out. The 'earnings rule' bears particularly hardly on them.

'Poorer, I am that', said the 53-year-old widow of a Scottish baker who had died on the operating table (29). 'I never got an awful big wage from my husband, but it was steady. I get £4 17s. 6d. to keep my daughter and me. Now I go out three days a week in the forenoon 9 to 11.' This courageous woman kept on her house by taking in a policeman as boarder; two of her sons were married, but the girl was still at school: 'No matter where her Dad went, she was with him. They [children] forget it though—maybe hide it.'

'I don't care what people say, money is very important,' said the 49-year-old widow of a professional man who had died in Rhodesia (62). 'I just have a very small pension. Well, abroad you spend money faster, so there was very little saved. . . . Financially, I had to go to work almost at once. Well, I got a job as a housekeeper in a place where I got a little cottage, but that place was foul; and I thought anyway there was far more life for children in a village like this [in Scotland] so this place came to my notice and I took it, and here we are. Children are fantastic, they just sort of bounce up.'

This woman had two boys, aged 12 and 9 when their father died. She came back to Britain for the children's sake, and because Rhodesia 'is definitely not a country for a woman alone.' Her elder boy wants to go into a bank 'so I'm quietly spending all the money I've got so I'll have nothing left.' She had never worked before in her life, but now had taken a full-time clerical job as

[2] Peter Marris: *Widows and Their Families.* Margaret Wynn: *Fatherless Families.*

clerkess. She was a woman of great courage—'I never cry, not about things about myself—I think this self-pity is ghastly.' She did, however, feel it was a stigma on herself and her children that she was living in a council house, because she could not find a suitable cottage to rent, though the house was a pleasant one.

This story of poverty was repeated by six other widows who were left with children of school age. To make ends meet, they all had to take jobs, chiefly unskilled and part-time (to avoid forfeiting their pensions under the earnings rule): delivering newspapers, cooking school lunches, office cleaning and the like. Most of them saw some secondary benefit from such jobs: 'You must occupy your mind with something else'; 'It's made a big difference to me; it started me off going out and about again' (11); 'I had to put a smile on' (21); and the like. These widows with young children felt they had a duty not to appear too sad and forlorn (in contrast to some of the mothers of slightly older children, who were beginning to achieve independence). 'I think when you've a family it's not fair to them to be that way [always sad] either. People don't want to come to your house when there's that kind of atmosphere, do they?' said the mother of two children in the North-West (21), who now works in a coal merchant's office.

Another problem which inevitably faces the widowed mother of young children was stated by a 49-year-old mother of two boys from the North-East (51) who has a full-time job as bus-conductress:

'You've got to be mother and father; and it's not the same; a woman can't talk to two young men as a man can. You've got to be very, very tactful. . . . They're two good lads, see. . . . Granted they like their own company, they're young people, they like to get out and that, but they're still here with me, like. . . . When this thing [widowhood] comes, you've just got to try to adapt yourself to different conditions. It is different, you've got no one of your own age you can talk to. When you've got young people you can't talk to them and tell them your troubles. When you've got a husband you can come home, can't you? and talk. There's definitely an emptiness.'

The absence of unguarded conversation—nobody to talk to—is of course one of the most noted deprivations of widowhood; but the presence of young children seems to render this more poignant, since you cannot just be silent but have to watch all the time what you say. The widow of a coal-merchant in Scotland (23) with two teen-aged daughters, whose husband died from a heart-attack, said:

'I've made a friend of a woman two years younger than me who lost her husband just a year after me—we're both the same—her husband is the same day as mine and her birthday the day before mine. So we go on holiday together. It's been a great help, you can sort of talk. You can't talk the same to the children. . . . It leaves an awful blank.'

This woman had to get a full-time job: 'I've two daughters, you see, one at school, one working.' Before her husband's death, 'I never really worked. . . . Only if I wanted something special I'd take a wee job for a wee while.' She was still in great distress: 'Och, I don't know, it takes longer to get over it; even yet I never really go out. There's not much fun left in life. I keep going because the girls have made me. Life's empty. . . . We used to go

to dances, but of course if I went now, I'd be the odd man
out. You do feel odd; you do feel out of it. Och aye, it's
hopeless . . . it's hopeless. . . . I do quite a bit of sewing
for my daughters.'

Although growing children add enormously to a widow's burden of responsibility, an invalid adult child seems
to give them an interest and occupation which dulls the
pain of widowhood. Three of my informants were or had
recently been in this situation: a 79-year-old woman in
the South-East (68) whose 52-year-old son was a mental
defective with a split palate who could only make hoot-
ing noises—the boy misses his father because he used to
take him for a daily walk; a 61-year-old widow in the Midlands (44) who cared for many years after her husband's
death for her spastic son; and the widow of a colliery
maintenance engineer who had a son stricken with polio
(34). Perhaps because these unfortunates demanded constant care and attention, these widows seemed less ha-
rassed than the mothers of growing children, and less
desolate than the mothers of healthy children who had
married and set up homes of their own.

Even among these widows there were some who paid
so much more attention to their role of mother than to
their role of wife, that their grief for the loss of their husband was submerged in the joy and pride in their children. Thus a gallant old lady of 85, living alone in the
South-West, who had lost her husband, a professional officer in the Services, after 63 years of marriage (22),
talked little of him or of her marriage, but was most volu-
ble about her children and grandchildren:

'Oh, it's a lonely time, but I have children and they
come in a lot; it eases things a bit. . . . I didn't sit and
cry—I'm not one of the weeping people; I've had to

take all kinds of things in my time. I've had children at death's door; and the doctors have said that it's nothing but skilful nursing and God's help that pulled them through. We never thought three of them would live; and now they're married, with families; that's nice, isn't it? . . . I think I've something to be proud of. They've all done well. I thank God for that because I think it's so nice, especially these days, there are so many queer people in the world, aren't there? I feel so glad that my children have turned out well; and people have said to me, "Well, your children have done well"; and I've prayed for them since the time they were born. . . . Well they have asked me [to go to live with them], but I think people are better on their own. When I go and stay with them I say, "Now, look here, if you want to go out, go out! I'm quite all right, give me something to read and the radio, not television, I can't stand that." . . . They are all nice to me. It's very nice to have them, when you hear people squabbling about their mother-in-law, and I don't think the mothers-in-law are always to blame! It's nice to look forward to seeing them; I make them laugh. It's nice to think they don't get bored with me! Oh! we're all good pals. . . . Well, my children say that they hope they're as active when they're my age; I'm 85 and until I had arthritis I could show them how to walk! Still, I might have had something worse, I suppose.'

Our conversation was a long one—it was a rainy afternoon and the old lady found it 'nice to have someone to talk to'; at the end of it I knew the detailed history of all her children and most of her grandchildren; but only two small incidents in her husband's life. She did not shy away from the subject, and answered any questions I asked; but all her thoughts were with her descendants.

She was fortunate in having many of her descendants round her; the 67-year-old widow of a retired senior civil servant, also in the South-West (31), had two sons to whom she was equally devoted; but their successful careers forced them to live abroad, one in Africa and the other in the United States. Her sitting-room was full of photographs of them, their homes and their children; after her husband's death she sold her car and visited her son in Africa: 'Since I came back I've been doing bed-and-breakfast; and now I've two boys from the technical college.' Because of these boarders she won't go yet to visit her son in America: 'I must think of them.' She was clearly giving them a mother's care; and, by so doing, was filling the emptiness of her life, avoiding the danger which she feared of 'getting morbid' and keeping busy.

'Keep busy; you've got to make a new life for yourself. . . . If I can help anyone I will do, but the only secret is to keep busy.'

The way in which many widows use keeping busy as a palliative of grief was detailed in the previous chapter (pp. 71–75).

The alternative to this busy-ness for widows who are childless or whose children are married and with establishments of their own, seems to be a lethargic, empty, solitary life in a house much too big for them, where they feed themselves inadequately and wait for death. This solitude, it would seem, is almost always self-chosen; 'The girls wanted me to give up the home; I wanted to keep my independence' (32); 'I'm trying to keep my home on, love, as long as I can. . . . My daughter wants me to live with them, but I don't want to break my little home up; not as long as I can keep it going' (35); 'I'd rather be alone than live with other people. It wouldn't be fair to my daughter to go to her.' (2) Eight widows, from all social classes and all parts of the country, made almost identical remarks. Only in one instance did I meet a widow who had chosen to live with her married daughter (1). (See p. 95.)

The emptiness of some of these widows' lives is appalling. 'I don't drink, and I don't smoke, and I don't go out. . . . I don't go in anybody's house, love; and nobody comes in mine, only my own family. . . . I like to be quiet, I'm not troublesome at all,' said the old lady (35) who was struggling to 'keep her little home' of a three-bedroom council house going on a pension supplemented by national assistance. 'It's £1 4s. 1d. this, and a bit of coal's ten and odd, only I'm careful and I don't go out much. I cook for myself just a bit. And every Sunday, I go to my daughter's. Lunch and tea.'

Often it seems as though this weekly or fortnightly visit is the only time these widows get a solid meal: 'I go to my husband's sister-in-law every Sunday and sit down to her table, so I get a cut off the joint.' (44)

Unless they're working full time these widows cannot, it would seem, be bothered to cook for themselves. They nearly all report a considerable loss of weight. And it is not only cooking they give up: 'I've never bothered to put any make-up on since my husband died; it just doesn't seem worth it,' said a 49-year-old widow from the South-East (36). Since she is just under 50, a generous government gives her a pension of 10s. of which 9s. 4d. goes back in insurance stamps. Her husband ran a flourishing car-hire business; when he died there was £1 in the post-office and 6s. 8d. in the bank. Luckily, this woman has a profession of her own. Another very recent widow from the Midlands (33) lost over 14 pounds in thirteen weeks: 'There's not much point in cleaning and keeping the house, really.' She has two daughters, one married and the other to be married in January, when she will be quite alone, except for her pets. She has a little bitch who's 'never left me. She's a stray, you know. She sleeps on my bed each night and I can feel a little bit of warmth at the bottom. You know.'

Another 10s. widow in the Midlands, who is quite alone except for a fortnightly visit from her married daughter, (2) had to take a job as a shop assistant; she had not worked during her marriage.

> 'I've got a home and a good fire; and when I get in I put the radio on, not to listen to, but because I can hear voices. . . . It was odd after the funeral; for ages I couldn't get the house warm. It was probably imagination. Just a coldness. There's something missing, of course; a big thing. I think if I'd have gone out of the house, I would never have come back. So I didn't have a holiday and made a point of not going away.'

Problems which all widows who lived alone with their husbands had to face after his death was whether to return at once to the desolate house or go away for a short holiday, and what to do with his personal possessions. Most of the widows went away for a week or so, typically to a married daughter; but I question whether this has much therapeutic value, and those who faced their empty house at once, frequently with a temporary visitor, seem to have managed to recover from intense grief sooner. Most widows sell or give away most of their husband's possessions (to their children if they are suitable for them), but many keep one personal relic, his watch, his favourite blazer (23) and the like.

A dilemma of which middle-class women are very conscious is the acceptance of social invitations. 'You miss the protection of marriage. It gives you an inferiority complex; you don't know if you're really welcome at all the places you've gone to. I can't relax like I used to,' said the very recent widow of a business-man in the Midlands (33).

'There's one thing you have to be careful of, if you're a widow; you have to be dreadfully careful if you've got friends with husbands; you feel you're butting in.' (44)

This is generally not a problem for working-class widows, who typically engage in a much less extensive social life among people who are not related in any way. The one exception are the younger widows (e.g. 23) who used to go to dances with their husbands.

Another marked class difference is the role that the late husband's family plays in the widow's life. With middle-class widows (23, 33, 36, 44) the husband's kin are frequently a greater source of support and company than are their own, particularly the husband's sisters or brothers; but this was only the case with one working-class informant (51), who said that her husband's sister was her best friend. Typically, working-class widows have little or no contact with their late husband's family; several (22, 29, 32, 34, 46, 68) say that they are not even sure what relatives of their husband are still alive. All but one of these informants come from the Southern half of England, where the working-class family is typically mother-centred; but even in the North and in Scotland the husband's kin play a minimal role in a working-class widow's life.

Only one of my informants had remarried (57). Her first marriage had taken place during the war and her husband was killed on the first anniversary of her wedding-day. Her grief then was so intense that she felt she had no tears left to shed (I was interviewing her about the

recent death of her parents). Her second marriage to a schoolmaster seemed very happy; she had three small children. The widow of the professional man who had died in Rhodesia (62) and who spoke with such frankness, said that she wasn't certain that 40 was not a better age to be widowed than 50, as a younger woman might have found life easier, and might be able to make a new one. Her marriage had obviously been a good one.

v Death of Wife

Two out of the nine widowers whom I interviewed had remarried (25, 63) within three years of their first wife's death, and a third had been on the verge of marrying the widow who attended to his housekeeping (47) when he found she was only wanting to exploit him. All three were men within a few years of 50, all worked in shops and, in each case, the wife had died of cancer. I have no reason to think the first marriages were not happy.

Widowerhood appears to pose three alternatives to British men: remarriage, withdrawal into a resigned depression, or removal to a new town and a new job. By November, 1963, several of the widowers whom I had hoped to talk to had left the addresses at which they were living in May of that year. Only one of the widowers whom I talked to who had not remarried seemed to be living a relatively comfortable life. This was a 55-year-old Local Government official in the South-East (42) who was living in cosy comfort with a housekeeper and an old dog; his wife had died five years earlier and his only daughter was married and living abroad.

This man received considerable help from his wife's mother and sister who live in the neighbourhood; they both stayed with him for a few days after the death of his

wife, and still visit him frequently and talk about his wife
to him. He felt that having them round him in the first
days after her death, so that he could not be on his own
as much as he felt he wanted to be, had been a considerable help in getting over the most acute phase of his grief.

'Living by myself and just thinking, I very very often
get round to it now, you know; something reminds you
. . . you can't stop, can you? You just don't pass over
them, do you? I don't think you should make that the
end of your life; you've got to carry on. You can't bury
yourself; no sense in that, is there? I'm sure they
wouldn't wish it.'

Burying themselves is an apt description of the behaviour of those desolate widowers (4, 41, 65) who, as
described in the last chapter (pp. 85–87) preserve their
houses as mausoleums to their dead wives, so that they
are metaphorically mummified. A man's status is not
changed, in Britain, by the loss of his wife in any way
analogous to that in which a woman's is changed by the
loss of her husband; his working life is not modified nor
his economic position worsened[3]; but for many men the
emotional burden of loneliness seems extremely heavy. As
a generalization it could be said that grief-stricken British
widows can find no reason or comfort in going out of
their house (save when they go to work); British widowers can find no reason or comfort in coming home.

The manufacturer in the North-West (65) tried to
avoid his mausoleum home, four years empty, by staying
at his place of work till two or three in the morning; he
seemed to me very near a breakdown. The cement-worker

[3] His allowances will be altered for income tax purposes; but if he
employs a housekeeper he will get an allowance for her; there is no
comparable arrangement for a widow.

in the South-East (41) was on night-shift; his waking
hours were taken up with keeping the house exactly as
his wife had left it, and his allotment and garden. He had
lost his wife suddenly fifteen months earlier after thirty-
four years of marriage. He still frequently sees her family,
since they live in the neighbourhood; but as far as his own
brothers are concerned 'we don't visit much, we never
have'.

'The loss—coming home and dinner on the table—
well, coming home to an empty house and getting your
own dinner it's—hard to start; but as I say, fifteen
months now. We were a long time together, you see.
. . . It's an empty life altogether, really. . . . Things
run just the same as she was here, with the neighbours
and that; they come along and everything seems, well,
as a matter of fact, normal; it's just that it's my feeling
that everything seems empty. When you walk in the
room and nobody's there, that's the worst part of it,
coming back.'

This man shared the tending of the house with his unmarried son; but since he was on night-shift and the son
on day-work with a two-hour journey each way, they were
seldom together except in the early evening and at week-
ends.

The 69-year-old retired stoker from the Midlands (4)
had been a widower for three years after forty-four years
of marriage. His house was full of his wife's clothes and
belongings; his one consolation was going to church and
visiting her grave three times a week. He was looked after
by one of his daughters who lived near; he had eight children and he could not reckon how many grandchildren,
but they were neither comfort nor company: 'I'm on my
own.' His house was cold and dark.

Retired widowers who want to 'keep their little home' rather than live with their married children are in an even worse case than are widows, for they tend to lack the simplest domestic skills.

'I am a member of an over-60 club, and that gives me an afternoon, you see, to put in; and the other days I'm occupied in the house . . . Cooking? I don't do much at all; anything will do for me.'

These are the words of a 66-year-old retired tracer from the North-East (58). He gets a little help from his sister-in-law who 'comes down occasionally; she's on her own as well'.

A 71-year-old retired factory worker in Scotland (30) had also joined a club since his wife died; indeed he was just leaving for the weekly meeting of the old timers' club for the old hands at the factory when I saw him. His children visit him occasionally for a week-end; otherwise he's by himself: 'I do all masel', shopping and that! . . . It's the company you miss . . . The house is empty.'

Both these houses were carefully tended, indeed spick and span; both were rather cold and comfortless. The house in the North-East looked big enough to have turned the upper storey into a flat, the solution adopted by a 48-year-old single-handed shopkeeper in the South-East (47) who let his rooms to a young couple upstairs; he joins them for meals. This was a fairly recent arrangement. For the first two years after his wife's death he had been looked after by a widow with an adolescent son; he had nearly married her, 'but I found out it wouldn't work in time'. He would like to marry again, if he could find the right woman:

'There's not much I can say; the only thing is you're terribly lonely. . . . She had a large family, and I don't have anything to do with them; we had differences. While she was in hospital my sister in —— came down to look after me and they resented it.'

This man reproached himself for 'moping' too much; but he had not surrendered to despair. 'Life's got to go on,' he repeated more than once; and if he can find a less venial woman than his former housekeeper he should be able to have a tolerable second marriage.

The two informants who had remarried had to be interviewed at their places of work, since their second wives, who in both cases had not known their predecessor, might have been upset. Both men had made formal mourning for their first wife. The business-man in the North-East (63) had performed the concentrated ritual of Orthodox Jewry (see pp. 79–80); the Scottish tradesman (25) had followed the less intense ritual of the Church of Scotland and had worn mourning and withdrawn from all social life for several weeks. Both still stay on good terms with their first wife's family. In the two-year interval before his second marriage the business-man from the North-East spent most of his leisure with a friend of his whose wife had also died of cancer at about the same time. They used to have weekly games of cards with two bachelors, resuming a practice dating from before his first marriage. Both men seemed to me to be contented and well adjusted.

vi *Death of Brother or Sister*

'Well it's surprising; we girls just cling together and the boys—we don't see much of them', (5) succinctly describes the typical relations between adult brothers and sisters in the British working classes and the emotions they are likely to feel when one of them dies. Sisters will grieve very deeply for sisters; but their brothers have gone out of their lives, and any mourning is likely to be formal. If brothers have kept contact with their brothers or sisters they will feel some grief; but typically men are absorbed into their wife's family at marriage and only meet their brothers and sisters intermittently at Christmas and similar family gatherings while their common mother is still alive. The chief exception to this generalization are those towns and villages where most of the men are employed in old-established industries such as mining (67), dock-work, shipbuilding and the like (38); in these communities all the brothers may be employed in the same mine or factory; in such cases the links between the brothers are close; the wives are absorbed into their husbands' family, and the links between sisters are not intense. As it happened, none of the people I interviewed in these communities had recently lost a brother or sister; the picture of the relationship between brothers and sisters was disclosed in the discussion of the effect of the death of a parent.

There is no analogous structuring of family relationships within the British middle classes. Here it is expected that adult brothers and sisters will be scattered, setting up or marrying into independent households whose whereabouts will be determined by considerations of employment or amenity rather than by proximity to a brother or sister. Affection or mourning for a brother or sister would seem in these classes to be chiefly determined by congeniality of character; I could find no consistent differences between the attitude of middle-class men and women to the deaths of their brothers or sisters. Compared with the working classes the affection between brothers seemed to be stronger, that between sisters less intense. If there is an unmarried or invalid brother or sister, the brothers will usually combine to care for this dependent after their parents' death.

A good statement of the middle-class view was given by the wife of a disabled officer in the South-East (26) who had lost her brother and sister within a couple of years of each other:

> 'The grief was for the fact that my brother and sister both died abnormally early, each at the age of 52 [from circulatory disease]. . . . I'm a good deal younger, you see, I was always the baby of the family. I feel it more in that way—in a sort of way I looked on them as kind of protectors against a harsh world. My sister was eleven years older than I and my brother nine years; so I can't help grieving that he went at 52. My brother did enjoy life. My sister was grieving for my mother; they were very close. I think my mother's death sent her off. . . . It was strange, at Mother's funeral she didn't cry at all; I was expecting her to weep buckets. I was struggling with tears, but she seemed totally unmoved. Well, one often hears that people who react like that are perhaps a great deal worse inside. I don't think she had anything much to live for after my mother died; she was never close to anyone after. I think it was heartbreak, though she did make an effort to smarten up her appearance. My brother did love life; I'm sure he didn't want to die.'

A technician in the North-East, who is very active in the Scout movement, lost two of his older brothers in the last year. They were, he said, very close, and he misses them a lot, particularly his eldest brother whom he often went round to see.

'If I meet any friends and we get talking, I point out the good points my brothers had; I like to praise them up like they were; they were all good lads.'

Neither of these informants admitted to feeling any apprehension for themselves following these deaths, perhaps because death from heart-failure is apparently painless.

A railway worker in the North-West (55) stated the more general working-class position:

'Well you've got to accept them [deaths] like. It'll always be happening; people will always be losing somebody. . . . They come to your mind; although you may not worry, you think about them. I think of my brothers and sisters . . . just in my mind.'

An old-age pensioner in the South-East (56) aged 68 lost two elder brothers and a younger sister within seven months:

'I used to run over to see the elder brother; I just miss that, and that's all there is about it . . . I accept the loss, that's all. . . . Well, you don't fall over; you remember them though. I've got sufficient sense to know you can go too far and have it on your nerves.'

A school-caretaker in the South-East about her sister (54):

'You see, I didn't see an awful lot of her; she was unmarried and had to go to business . . . she was doing a job and was taken ill and that was it.'

A van-driver from the South-West (43) about his unmarried sister aged 66, who had died in his home:

'She'd travelled round quite a bit, then she lived with one of the family; she was the eldest sister and had no home of her own, so resided with a sister or brother, you see. . . . I look on it like this, you can't bring her back to life, can you? It was our eldest sister, and naturally you don't get used to it for a long time. . . . We're quite happy in our way to think that we've done everything we could for her, and, as I say we can't get her back.'

Besides the informant there were also present in the room and taking part in the interview his elder brother, his wife, his daughter, his baby grandson and his aged aunt; also a cat, a budgerigar and a large TV set going full blast. All those capable of speech chipped in at one time or another; and I got the impression that the one person who was deeply attached to the dead woman and mourned her was her niece, who still dreams of her frequently: 'She was always so friendly to us all.'

A butcher in the Midlands was sad when his widowed sister died; he had a lot of worry with her death because all her children were married and living away; but it is the children who arranged for the burial and tend the grave. He didn't make any show of grief; he 'likes to bottle everything up.'

In contrast, the 65-year-old wife of a toolgrinder in the South-East was so distressed by the death of her younger sister that she can't concentrate; she feels she will never get over it. She has got her older sister living with her, and the two old ladies are in a very sad state indeed. The most touching account of the grief for a loss of a younger sister was that given by the wife of the pensioned bricklayer in the South-East (37).

'It was a very bad loss to me; I felt it very bad when she went. It's no good crying over it now, not a bit; it won't bring her back. I still remember her as she was, of course. I'll tell you one thing about it; the hospital was very good to her, the doctor was beautiful and the nurses; she was well looked after, and if they could have saved her they would have done. . . . I remember her when she was a baby. . . . I dream about her too; she often comes to me, you know, we have a laugh and that, we're always together and working in my dreams. . . . We was all sociable girls together and we all helped one another. If there was a beggar on the road I'd give him a loaf and go without myself. I mean I've had hard times; I haven't always had it easy. I know what it was to go to the pawnshop to feed my children. . . . Oh, lovely help the neighbours was, so was the hospital, beautiful help. She worked up there fourteen years; they thought the world of her.'

vii *Death of Child*

The most distressing and long-lasting of all griefs, it would seem, is that for the loss of a grown child. In such a case it seems to be literally true, and not a figure of speech, that the parents never get over it. I can only speculate as to why this should be so, for most of my informants were not very articulate. First, it would appear that, at least in time of peace, it is 'against the order of nature' that a child should die before his or her parents; and it seems as though the parents, in some obscure way, interpret this as a punishment for their own shortcomings, a sort of divine retribution, whether they are actively religious or no. Second, although a person's social status is in no way modified by the death of a grown child, it seems as though their self-image may be destroyed; the more they have thought of themselves as primarily mother or father, and only secondarily as husband or wife, as exercising some skill or profession, the more shattering a blow it can be. This is of course most clearly the case with a widow or widower with an only child; but a similar mechanism seems to be involved even when both spouses are living and other children survive. Perhaps a reliance on the orderliness of the universe has been undermined.

Pious Roman Catholics can still do something for their children's welfare by having Masses said for the repose of their souls; this was some consolation to an old-age pensioner on National Assistance in the North-East (66) who saved a little from his pittance to have Masses said for his boy who was killed in a motor-cycle accident when he was 22 years old: 'It's got to be my sacrifice.' The boy had a twin brother who was badly injured in the same accident; but he has recovered, married and moved to another part of the country. The old father is quite alone—his wife had died shortly before the accident—and, he said, completely without friends; he does his own cleaning and shopping. He had a certain resigned dignity—'Be of good heart. Don't rely on other people'—but seemed quite without hope; he thinks of his boy all the time. He was sitting in the dark with the flames from a good fire flickering on his son's photograph.

An obviously diabetic woman in Scotland has a Mass said on the anniversary of the death of her daughter; she died at the age of 45 from a brain-tumour; but her mother hopes and trusts that she made a last confession and died fortified by the rites of the Church. This daughter was married, with five children, three of them grown up; the father looks after the younger ones. Besides the daughter who died, she has another daughter living near who was present with one of her grandchildren when I called, and three sons, one in the forces, one in the Merchant Navy and one in the U.S.A. But 'I still feel it yet, you know—I couldn't realize it. They always came down to see me, no matter what happened. . . . It was a big blow.' She could still hardly bear to talk about it.

A woman in South-East England (3) could not keep the tears out of her voice when she talked of her niece, her adoptive daughter, who had gassed herself more than three years previously because she was suffering from acromegaly:

> 'I grieve terribly. . . . You can't help grieving, but you don't have to let it overpower your life. . . . I don't want anyone to think I'm sitting down grieving; but occasionally it does come up, and then I start work— I'm a real worker, and then I get on with it. . . . We've reached the age of three score and ten and when the time comes, we shall go; I've no fears, I'm ready.'

The same tearfulness choked the voice of an old lady in the North-West (49) when she talked about her younger boy who had died 'of kidneys' three years previously; the elder son and two daughters were still living, but 'he were a lovely boy; he never hurt a soul'. They had recently moved into a new area, in part it would seem to get away from people who had known the son: 'There are things you can't ever forget. . . .'

This son had left a young widow and an 11-year-old daughter; she had recently remarried. Before making the engagement official she and her intended had come to ask her mother-in-law's approval. 'So I took it best way I could.' The daughter-in-law and the granddaughter still make a monthly visit.

A professional man, now living in the South-West (53) had lost his 15-year-old boy while he was living in the North.

'He left school on the Wednesday and went out playing on the Thursday; and whilst he was playing there
were some boys throwing stones at tin cans. He ran
between them and got struck on the forehead with a
stone, the result being of course that it caused instant
death; and the lads ran away and left him there, and it
wasn't discovered till about an hour and a half later.
. . . They had to phone me at work. It was a big shock.
It takes everything out of you for the moment. You
get a kind of numbness and you do things automati-
cally; you know you have certain things to do and you
kind of do them without—well, with a kind of hazy
feeling all the time. . . . Sometimes you see or hear
something which reminds you, and it comes up a wee
bit. You're not conscious of it until something comes
along to remind you. . . . I do sometimes going along
perhaps see some lad that is like him, like he was, and
it makes you just think for a moment, you know; spe-
cially as he was a very peculiar laddie, he wore glasses,
and he would insist on wearing one lens lower than the
other; and sometimes I see a lad with specs like that,
and it just reminds you. . . . He was due to go into a
nautical school down South.'

This man had been separated from the boy's mother before this death occurred; she was a member of Jehovah's
Witnesses and at the funeral her family and friends 'instead of being any comfort, they turned their back on
me; they wouldn't even shake hands. I went to shake
hands and they ignored me . . . to hold out your hand
to an individual is embarrassing.' He is now remarried, it
would seem happily enough, with a stepson and a little
daughter.

'After it happened I didn't want to live,' said the widow

of a Midlands business-man (44) about the death of her
spastic son.

'I have to put his last few weeks away out of my
mind, otherwise my inside's in a turmoil. His Daddy
died without pain, whereas—J. had a lot of pain.
There's been a lot of love, J. brought a lot to us. I've
made a completely different life now. . . . For three
years I couldn't bear the thought of going where we
used to live, but now I can face it. . . . To a point,
you sometimes think, "Why should it happen?"; but
then you mix with people who've had a worse time
than you. [I don't go to church because] I'm afraid
I'm rather emotional; I get a lump; I think of the last
hours of J. . . . I don't give vent to tears. . . . After
it happened, I didn't want to live, I didn't take an
interest in people; but my husband left me a legacy of
friendship. Friendship—it's something you've got to
fight for yourself, as well. I didn't want to live. But I've
got something to say about [city] welfare. I'm glad that
I live in the age of the kindness of [the city]—their
visitors. And also our burden was less with radio. That
helped a lot with J., that was his life—the radio. Living
in this age one has such a lot of help in different ways.'

I did not feel that there was anything theatrical in this
woman's despair; with her son's death, her life had become meaningless. The widow of a baker in Scotland (29)
whose husband had died on the operating table when he
was about 50 years old said, 'Funny thing, his mother
died five weeks after him; she was heartbroken.'

The death of infants or young children does not seem
to have anything like the same emotional impact. The
two parents I spoke to who had suffered this loss dis-
missed it in a few factual sentences; in neither case were

they only children. The wife of the railway worker from the North-West (55) said of their daughter:

'She's a hard-hearted girl, isn't she? She's sensible. She lost two babies—one was 36 hours and the other a week. . . . But she doesn't brood. . . . [She has no living children.] Not yet. They've a beautiful home, everything they could wish for; it's just one of them things, you see, you have to accept.'

In contrast, the wife of a Midlands assistant sales manager (6) said of her sister:

'My youngest lost her five-year-old boy the year before [their father died]. Kidney trouble. My sister went berserk, she went haywire. She didn't believe it, it was so sudden. . . . She started to smoke, and has about twenty a day now; she was that upset.'

My informant had herself given up smoking for three months, after the death of her father, as a form of mourning.

CONCLUSIONS

I think that the material presented has adequately demonstrated that the majority of British people are today without adequate guidance as to how to treat death and bereavement and without social help in living through and coming to terms with the grief and mourning which are the inevitable responses in human beings to the death of someone whom they have loved. The minority who are convinced adherents of religious creeds or sects have the assistance and comfort provided by the traditions and eschatology of their religions and (in some cases) by the social ritual which is interwoven with the religious practices; and members of such modern movements as Spiritualism, Christian Science, and European or American adaptations of Asian religions have at least the support of their fellow dogmatists in their denial of the 'reality' or importance of death and their refusal to admit mourning.

It has also been demonstrated that only a minority of the British are active in the practice of their religion—less than a third attend a religious service once a month, and less than a half say daily prayers; consequently, the fact that the only social techniques available for coming to terms with death and dealing with grief are phrased exclusively in religious terms means that the majority of contemporary Britons with either residual or non-existent religious beliefs have in effect neither help nor guidance in the crises of misery and loneliness which are likely to occur in every person's life. I think my material illustrates the hypothesis that this lack of accepted ritual and guidance is accompanied by a very considerable amount of maladaptive behaviour, from the triviality of meaningless 'busy-ness' through the private rituals of what I have called mummification to the apathy of despair.

To the best of my knowledge, there is no analogue from either the records of past societies or the description of present societies outside the Judeo-Christian tradition to this situation in which the majority of the population lack common patterns or ritual to deal with the crises inherent in man's biological nature. Within societies deriving from the Judeo-Christian tradition there is a faint analogue in the confusions concerning appropriate sexual behaviour. With sex, too, the traditional patterns and ritual have been phrased in religious terms and controlled by sanctions justified by scriptural authority; and the majority who pay at most lip-service to the authority of the scriptures have had to develop their own lay patterns and ethics, often at considerable psychological cost.

The problem of dealing with sex in secular terms has been discussed with increasing clarity for the better part of a century. Although there is still no complete consensus on the most appropriate social ways of dealing with sexual urges, there is now a very general recognition that human beings do have sexual urges and that, if these are denied outlet, the result will be suffering, either psychological or physical or both. But there is no analogous secular recognition of the fact that human beings mourn in response to grief, and that, if mourning is denied outlet, the result will be suffering, either psychological or physical or both. At present death and mourning are treated with much the same prudery as sexual impulses were a century ago. Then it was held, quite sincerely, that good women, or ladies, had no sexual impulses, and that good men, or gentlemen, could keep theirs under complete control by strength of will or character. Today it would seem to be believed, quite sincerely, that sensible, rational men and women can keep their mourning under complete control by strength of will or character so that it need be given no public expression, and indulged, if at all, in private, as furtively as if it were an analogue of masturbation. The gratitude with which a number of my informants thanked me for talking to them without embarrassment about their grief—a typical phrase was 'I've got a lot off my chest'—must, I think, be similar to the gratitude felt a couple of generations earlier by people when their sexual secrets could finally be discussed without prudery or condemnation.

There is not, as yet, sufficient information available to determine the 'normal' pattern of mourning by adults; but judging by my interviews and the range of rituals and practices reported by historians and anthropologists, it would seem as though most adult mourners pass through three stages: a short period of shock, usually lasting between the occurrence of death and the disposal of the body; a period of intense mourning accompanied by the withdrawal of much attention and affect from the external world and by such physiological changes as disturbed and restless sleep, often with vivid dreams, failure of appetite and loss of weight; and a final period of reestablished physical homeostasis—sleep and weight again stabilized and interest again directed outward.

The first period of shock is, it would appear, generally given social recognition. Kinsfolk gather round the mourners for the family gatherings, religious ceremonies and, often, ritual meals in Britain, as has been described in earlier chapters; and, in the United States, the curious elaborations of the morticians, with overtones of religiosity,[1] are concentrated on this period. Once the funeral, and possibly the post-funereal meal, are finished, the ritual which might give support to the bereaved is finished too, and they are left to face the period of intense mourning without either support or guidance.

The traditional customs of Britain, of all European countries and of very many societies outside the Judeo-Christian tradition prescribe usually in great detail the costume and behaviour appropriate to mourners in the period of intense mourning after the funeral; they also typically impose an etiquette on all those who come in

---

[1] See, for example, Evelyn Waugh, *The Loved One*; Jessica Mitford, *The American Way of Death*; Ruth Mulvey Harmer, *The High Cost of Dying*.

contact with the mourners; and usually designate the number of days, weeks, months or years that this behaviour should be followed. It is this pattern which I dubbed 'time-limited mourning'; and, on the basis of comparative material from other societies, from the findings of psychoanalysis, and from the material presented in the foregoing pages, it would appear to be the most appropriate technique for mourners to make the complicated psychological and social adjustments involved in the loss of a primary relative. If these adjustments are not made, the outcome is liable to be either the permanent despair of depression or melancholia, an impairment of the capacity to love in the future, or various irrational attitudes towards death and destruction. Some of the possible irrational developments of denied mourning will be discussed subsequently.

The material presented in the foregoing pages, (and, I believe, most people's personal experience) demonstrates that the most typical reaction of the majority in Britain today (and, as far as my evidence goes, in all English-speaking countries with a Protestant tradition) is the denial of mourning, in the period after the funeral. Certainly, social recognition of mourning has practically disappeared; we no longer recognize a mourner when we see one—a black tie may be worn for its elegance, without any symbolic intent—and are at a loss and embarrassed when we do consciously meet one. Giving way to grief is stigmatized as morbid, unhealthy, demoralizing—very much the same terms are used to reprobate mourning as were used to reprobate sex; and the proper action of a friend and well-wisher is felt to be distraction of a mourner from his or her grief; taking them 'out of themselves' by diversions, encouraging them to seek new scenes and experiences, preventing them 'living in the past'.

Mourning is treated as if it were a weakness, a self-indulgence, a reprehensible bad habit instead of as a psychological necessity.

Many people, of course, can adjust to this public attitude by treating it as if it were an extension of modesty;
one mourns in private as one undresses or relieves oneself
in private, so as not to offend others; and this is probably
the best solution now available. But there are many, I
believe, who accept the implications of the current social
attitude uncritically and deny their feelings of mourning
to themselves, as well as in public, and fight against giving
them any expression as they fight against giving way to
reprehended sensual indulgences. This conscious refusal
to mourn would seem to have a number of socially undesirable developments.

If one can deny one's own grief, how much more easily
can one deny the grief of others; and one possible outcome of the public denial of mourning is a great increase
in public callousness. That this has occurred seems
probable but impossible to document; the changed techniques of mass communication have so enlarged the world
in which most people live that increased callousness may
be the only possible response to the ever-increasing
amount of misery and cruelty of which one is informed.
I would, however, be inclined to consider that the resignation, indeed complacency, with which the daily toll of
death and mutilations by the automobile is accepted, is a
sign of an increase in callousness which is, at any rate,
contemporaneous with the decrease in the admissibility
of mourning.

An aspect of callousness—the opposite face of it—is
excessive squeamishness about references to death, pain
or mourning, treating these human experiences as though
they were obscene, so that any mention or depiction of

them is considered unpleasant for the mature and cor-
rupting for the immature. The constant complaints about
the depiction of 'violence' on television or cinema screen
are as symptomatic as the preoccupation with death and
cruelty in the 'horror films', and 'horror comics' and the
endless spate of ill-written paper-back books on the hor-
rors of war and concentration camps. The 'pornography
of death', whether it be furtively enjoyed or self-righ-
teously condemned, manifests an irrational attitude towards death and a denial of mourning.

Another contemporary preoccupation which I would
tend to link with the denial of mourning is the excessive
preoccupation with the risk of death which is given public
expression in many of the activities of those agitating
against nuclear warfare and, more recently, with the risks
involved in cigarette smoking. No responsible person can
fail to consider a nuclear war as the greatest potential
peril that the human species has ever faced; but it is the
human species which is threatened and no localized population can contract out of the peril by demonstrations.
The connection between cigarette smoking and cancer of
the lung does seem to be statistically established; possibly other causes of death are less painful; but implicit in
quite a lot of the agitation to stop the sale or advertise-
ment of cigarettes is the suggestion that, without this
indulgence, people would be immortal. *Timor mortis con-
turbat me* was originally an expression of the fears of
posthumous Judgment on the part of the believing Christian; today it seems to be the motto of many tender-
minded agnostics.

Another contemporary manifestation which I would
tend to link with the denial of mourning is the increase in
'vandalism', in the destruction or mutilation of property
for the sake of destruction, without any rational consid-

eration of gain or of personal revenge being involved. The connection between vandalism and the denial of mourning is not quite so direct as is the connection with callousness or irrational preoccupation with, or fear of, death, for it takes into consideration an aspect of mourning which is given no overt expression in our culture. This aspect is the anger felt against the dead for abandoning the survivors.

Although our culture gives no symbolic expression to this anger, a considerable number of others have done so, by such rituals as the destruction of the dead person's property or possessions or, slightly more indirectly, by the various mutilations which mourners have to inflict on themselves as a sign of the pain which the dead have caused them. According to some psycho-analysts[2] this anger is a component of all mourning; and one of the main functions of the mourning process is to 'work through' and dissipate this anger in a symbolic and, to a great extent, unconscious fashion.

In psycho-analytic theory, if this anger is not worked through in mourning it will turn in on itself and result in the self-reproach and self-punishment which are the most marked symptoms of melancholia. But it seems to me possible that, perhaps particularly in the case of adolescents, such anger may be neither discharged nor turned in on the self; if adolescents are not able, or not allowed, to mourn (typically, for the loss of a parent by death or separation) it may be that this anger is, as it were, kept in suspense to be discharged as occasion offers by the gleeful destruction of insentient objects. I am informed that there is some evidence to suggest that lads committed to Borstals and similar institutions for wanton and apparently unmotivated destruction have a greater number of

[2] See Appendix One.

dead or disappeared parents, for whom it would have been appropriate to mourn, than do their fellows confined for 'rational' crimes such as theft. The validity of this hypothesis could be fairly easily determined by research, if the proper facilities were given.

If I am right in tracing a connection between the denial of mourning and callousness, irrational preoccupation with and fear of death, and vandalism, then it would seem correct to state that a society which denies mourning and gives no ritual support to mourners is thereby producing maladaptive and neurotic responses in a number of its citizens. And this further suggests the desirability of making social inventions which will provide secular mourning rituals for the bereaved, their kin and their friends and neighbours.

Such rituals must be basically secular, though they could be elastic enough to comprise religious components for the pious minority. But the fact that there has been no invention of 'civil mourning' analogous to the invention of 'civil marriage' may well have contributed to the denial of mourning by the majority of the population who have residual or no religious beliefs. Such rituals would have to take into account the need of the mourner for both companionship and privacy; for the fact that it is (almost certainly) desirable for mourners to give expression to their grief without embarrassment or reticence; and for the fact that for some weeks after bereavement a mourner is undergoing much the same physical changes as occur during and after a severe illness. The period of intense mourning probably varies with the temperament of the mourner and the nature of the relationship with the deceased; my impression is that the median range is between six and twelve weeks. During this period the mourner is in more need of social support and assistance than at any time since infancy and early childhood; and at the moment our society is signally failing to give this support and assistance. The cost of this failure in misery, loneliness, despair and maladaptive behaviour is very high.

APPENDIX ONE

CURRENT AND RECENT THEORIES
OF MOURNING AND THE PRESENT
MATERIAL

One short essay by Freud—*Mourning and Melancholia*, written in 1915 and published in 1917[1]—dominates all the psycho-analytical and most of the psychiatric and sociological studies of grief and mourning written since that date. Much of the later work is in the nature of exegesis on this text. A question which is much discussed, but which I will not comment on, is whether the description of the mourning process

[1] Bibliographical details of the books and articles quoted in this appendix, and in the body of the book, are given on pp. 200–1. For permission to quote from copyright material I am grateful to Dr. John Bowlby and the *International Journal of Psycho-Analysis* for allowing me to quote from 'The Processes of Mourning', published in Volume XLII of the Journal in 1960; to Dr. Thomas D. Eliot and D. C. Heath & Co., Boston, for the extract from *Family, Marriage and Parenthood*; to Dr. G. Engel and the Hoeber Medical Division, Harper & Row, New York, for the extract from 'Is Grief a Disease?' from *Psychosomatic Medicine*, Volume III (1961); to Dr. H. Feifel and the McGraw-Hill Book Company, New York, for extracts from 'Attitudes towards Death in some Normal and Mentally Ill Populations' from *The Meaning of Death* (1959); to the executors of Sigmund Freud, the Hogarth Press, Mr. James Strachey, and Basic Books Inc., New York, for the extracts from 'Mourning and Melancholia' from *The Complete Psychological Works of Sigmund Freud*, Standard Edition, Volume 14; to the executors of Mrs. Melanie Klein, the Hogarth Press, and the McGraw-Hill Book Company, New York, for the excerpt from 'Mourning and Its Relation to Manic-Depressive States' from *Contributions to Psycho-Analysis, 1921–45*; to Dr. Eric Lindemann and the American Psychiatric Association for extracts from 'Symptomatology and Management of Acute Grief' from the *American Journal of Psychiatry*, Volume CI, 1944; and to Mr. Peter Marris and Routledge & Kegan Paul Ltd., for the extract from *Widows and Their Families*, 1958.

which Freud gives is applicable as a description of the unhappiness of infants and very young children at weaning or
when separated either temporarily or permanently from
their mothers.

Since this essay has been so influential, it is perhaps worth
stressing that Freud's major aim in writing it was to develop
hypotheses concerning the pathological condition of melancholia; the relatively few sentences on the 'normal emotion
of grief' are intended as points of contrast with the pathological state. Nor, as far as is known, were Freud's observations on normal mourning drawn from patients in psycho-
analysis; and his own life till that date[2] had been so free of
bereavement—his father had died at the age of 81 in 1896
and his half-brother Emanuel at the same age in 1914—that
it seems improbable that he relied much on introspection
or self-analysis. His description of mourning is based on his
wisdom rather than his observations; and his explanations are
hypotheses derived from the current stage of the developing
theories of psycho-analysis. Almost at the end of the essay he
recalls to his readers: 'We do not even know the economic
means by which mourning carries out its task.'

Since the wise observations on normal mourning are so
short, I propose quoting them at length.

'Mourning is regularly the reaction to the loss of a loved
person, or to the loss of some abstraction which has taken
the place of one, such as one's country, liberty, an ideal,
and so on. In some people the same influences produce
melancholia instead of mourning and we consequently suspect them of a pathological disposition. It is also well
worth notice that, although mourning involves grave de-
partures from the normal attitude to life, it never occurs
to us to regard it as a pathological condition and to refer
it to medical treatment. We rely on its being overcome
after a certain lapse of time, and we look upon any inter-
ference with it as useless and even harmful. . . .

[2] Ernest Jones: *Sigmund Freud: Life and Work*, Vols. I and II.

'Profound mourning, the reaction to the loss of someone who is loved, contains the same painful frame of mind, the same loss of interest in the outside world—in so far as it does not recall him—the same loss of capacity to adopt any new object of love (which would mean replacing him) and the same turning away from any activity that is not connected with thoughts of him. It is easy to see that this inhibition and circumscription of the ego is the expression of an exclusive devotion to mourning which leaves nothing over for other purposes or other interests. It is really only because we know so well how to explain it that this attitude does not seem to us pathological. . . .

'In what, now, does the work which mourning performs consist? I do not think there is anything far-fetched in presenting it in the following way. Reality-testing has shown that the loved object no longer exists, and it proceeds to demand that all libido shall be withdrawn from its attachment to that object. This demand arouses understandable opposition—it is a matter of general observation that people never willingly abandon a libidinal position, not even, indeed, when a substitute is already beckoning to them. This opposition can be so intense that a turning away from reality takes place and a clinging to the object through the medium of a hallucinatory wishful psychosis. Normally, respect for reality gains the day. Nevertheless its orders cannot be obeyed at once. They are carried out bit by bit, at great expense of time and cathectic energy, and in the meantime the existence of the lost object is psychically prolonged. Each single one of the memories and expectations in which the libido is bound to the object is brought up and hypercathected, and detachment of the libido is accomplished in respect of it. Why this compromise by which the command of reality is carried out piecemeal should be extraordinarily painful is not at all easy to explain in terms of economics. It is remarkable that this painful unpleasure is taken as a matter of course by us. The fact is, however, that when the work

of mourning is completed the ego becomes free and un-
inhibited again.

'We found . . . that in mourning time is needed for the
command of reality-testing to be carried out in detail, and
that when this work has been accomplished the ego will
have succeeded in freeing its libido from the lost object.'

It was during the miseries and anxieties of the First World
War that Freud directed his attention to death and mourning; it was at the beginning of the Second, in 1940, that
Melanie Klein published her major commentary on this text,
Mourning and Its Relation to Manic-Depressive States. The
dominant theme in this paper is the elaboration of Mrs.
Klein's psycho-analytic version of predestination, of the
phases through which human infants are doomed to pass, in
particular the second crisis of the 'depressive position'. This
depressive position is described as inevitable and based on
phantasies:

'When the depressive position arises, the ego is forced
. . . to develop methods of defence which are essentially
directed against the "pining" for the loved object. These
are fundamental to the whole ego-organisation. . . . The
ego is driven by depressive anxieties (anxiety lest the loved
objects as well as itself should be destroyed) to build up
omnipotent and violent phantasies. . . .'

With this hypothesised infantile experience it is understandable that Mrs. Klein contends that

'the child goes through states of mind comparable to
the mourning of the adult, or rather, that this early mourning is revived whenever grief is experienced in later life.
. . . We have now to connect the infantile depressive position with normal mourning. The poignancy of the actual
loss of a loved person is, in my view, greatly increased by
the mourner's unconscious phantasies of having lost his
internal "good" objects as well. He then feels that his in-

ternal "bad" objects predominate and his inner world is in
danger of disruption. . . . In normal mourning early psy-
chotic anxieties are reactivated. The mourner is in fact ill,
but because this state of mind is common and seems so
natural to us, we do not call mourning an illness. . . . To
put my conclusion more precisely: I should say that in
mourning the subject goes through a modified and transi-
tory manic-depressive state and overcomes it, thus repeating, though in different circumstances and with different
manifestations, the processes which the child normally goes
through in his early development.'

These hypotheses are, I would consider, not capable of
proof or disproof; it is a question of faith rather than of
evidence. In illustration of her hypotheses, Mrs. Klein recounts and interprets a few dreams from two bereaved people whom she had analysed—a mother who had lost a schoolboy son, and a middle-aged man who had lost his mother;
the mother-son relationship is, in Mrs. Klein's view, the basic
familial relationship. In the course of these descriptions, Mrs.
Klein makes some generalizations, chiefly in parenthesis,
which do allow of testing against observation.

'His [the mourner's] hatred of the loved person is increased by the fear that by dying the loved one was seek-
ing to inflict punishment and deprivation upon him, just as
in the past he felt that his mother, whenever she was away
from him and he wanted her, had died in order to inflict
punishment and deprivation on him.'
'In mourning as well as in infantile development, inner
security comes about not by a straightforward movement
but in waves.'
'If the mourner has people whom he loves and who
share his grief, and if he can accept their sympathy, the
restoration of the harmony in his inner world is promoted,
and his fears and distresses are more quickly reduced.'
'. . . people who fail to experience mourning. Feeling
incapable of saving and securely reinstating their loved

objects inside themselves, they must turn away from them more than hitherto and therefore deny their love for them. This may mean that their emotions in general become more inhibited; in other cases it is mainly feelings of love which beome stifled and hatred is increased.'

The last two observations, in particular, correspond with findings in the present study (pp. 61, 68).

In 1944 Dr. Eric Lindemann published a short paper entitled *Symptomatology and Management of Acute Grief* which is, to the best of my knowledge, the first and still the most complete analysis of the behaviour of recently bereaved persons. His findings were based on 101 patients divided into four categories; (1) psychoneurotic patients who lost a relative during the course of treatment; (2) relatives of patients who died in hospital; (3) relative of members of the armed forces; and (4) bereaved disaster victims. There was a terrible fire in a restaurant called Cocoanut Grove, in which many people perished; there were also some survivors, and thirteen of these are included in Dr. Lindemann's sample; typically one partner of a marriage had survived the other. Although these disaster victims represent only an eighth of the total sample reported on, they are quoted far more than the remaining seven-eighths and seem to have been very influential in Dr. Lindemann's picture of bereavement.

Dr. Lindemann opens his paper by listing three points he wishes to make: '(i) Acute Grief is a definite syndrome with psychological and somatic symptomatology; (ii) the syndrome may appear immediately after a crisis; it may be delayed; it may be exaggerated or apparently absent; (iii) in place of the typical syndrome there may appear distorted pictures, each of which represents one special aspect of the grief syndrome.'

Dr. Lindemann describes the symptomatology of normal grief as follows:[3]

[3] I have considerably abbreviated, but I hope not distorted, his description.

'The picture shown by persons in acute grief is remarkably uniform. Common to all is the following syndrome: sensations of somatic distress occurring in waves lasting from 20 minutes to an hour at a time, a feeling of tightness in the throat, choking with shortness of breath, need for sighing, and an empty feeling in the abdomen, lack of muscular power, and an intense subjective distress described as tension or mental pain. The patient soon learns that these waves of discomfort can be precipitated by visits, by mention of the deceased, and by receiving sympathy. There is a tendency to avoid the syndrome at any cost, to refuse visits lest they should precipitate the reaction, and to keep deliberately from thought all references to the deceased.

'Another strong preoccupation is with feelings of guilt. The bereaved searches the time before the death for evidence of failure to do right by the lost one. He accuses himself of negligence and exaggerates minor omissions.

'In addition there is often a disconcerting loss of warmth in relationship to other people, a tendency to respond with irritation and anger, a wish not to be bothered by others at a time when friends and relatives make a special effort to keep up friendly relationships.

'These feelings of hostility, surprizing and quite inexplicable to the patients, disturbed them and were again often taken as signs of approaching insanity. Great efforts are made to handle them, and the result is often a formalized, stiff manner of social interaction.

'The activity throughout the day of the severely bereaved person shows remarkable change. There is no retardation of action and speech; quite to the contrary there is a push of speech, especially when talking about the deceased. There is restlessness, inability to sit still, moving about in an aimless fashion, continually searching for something to do. There is, however, at the same time, a painful lack of capacity to initiate and maintain organized patterns of activity. What is done is done with lack of zest, as though one were going through the motions. The bereaved clings to the daily routine of prescribed activities; but these activities do not proceed in the automatic self-sustaining fashion which characterizes normal work but have to be carried on with effort, as though each fragment of the activity became a special task. The bereaved is surprized to find how large a part of this customary activity was done in some meaningful relationship to the deceased and has now lost its significance. Especially the habits of social interaction—meeting friends, making conversation, sharing enterprises with others—seem to have been lost.

'These five points—(1) somatic distress, (2) preoccupation with the image of the deceased, (3) guilt, (4) hostile reactions and (5) loss of patterns of conduct—seem to be pathognomic of grief. There may be added a sixth characteristic, shown by patients who border on pathological reactions . . . this is the appearance of traits of the deceased in the behaviour of the bereaved.

'The duration of a grief reaction seems to depend upon the success with which a person does the *grief work*, namely emancipation from the bondage of the deceased, readjustment to the environment in which the deceased is missing, and the formation of new relationships. One of the big obstacles to this work seems to be the fact that many patients try to avoid the intense distress connected with the grief experience and to avoid the expression of emotion necessary for it. The men victims after the Cocoanut Grove fire appeared in the early psychiatric interviews to be in a state of tension with tightened facial musculature, unable to relax for fear they might "break down". It required considerable persuasion to yield to the grief process before they were willing to accept the discomfort of bereavement.'

Besides the normal grief reactions Dr. Lindemann describes morbid grief reactions under two major categories: (*a*) Delay of Reaction—'the most striking and most frequent reaction of this sort is *delay* or *postponement*' and (*b*) Distorted Reactions. He lists nine of these: overactivity without a sense of loss; the acquisition of symptoms belonging to the last illness of the deceased; a recognized medical disease; alteration in relationship to friends and relatives; furious hostility against specific persons; hiding hostility but becoming wooden and formal; lasting loss of patterns of social interaction; activities detrimental to his own social and economic position (such as gross extravagance); and agitated depression.

I will postpone a discussion of those reactions listed by Dr. Lindemann which were not apparent in my material until later in this appendix.

Two other American students of grief may be mentioned more briefly. In 1955 Dr. Thomas D. Eliot contributed a chapter to the symposium *Family, Marriage and Parenthood* which he entitled *Bereavement: Inevitable but not insurmountable*. As with Dr. Lindemann, the bereavement he envisages is primarily the loss of a spouse; there is some mention of loss of parents, but practically none of brothers, sisters or children. At the beginning of his chapter Dr. Eliot writes:

'Bereavements are usually unexpected, often a shock, and seldom planned for either personally or by the family. . . . That bereavement has been so little studied can be attributed to inertia, taboo, and inherent methodological difficulties, not to the obscurity of the problem.'

Dr. Eliot's chapter has little theoretical or methodological consistency. There is a good deal of anecdote, with a surprisingly large number of illustrations and comments from Christian Scientists; he counsels rather than analyses. He does however have one paragraph about ritual, which is exceptional in the literature under discussion.

' "Something to be done" ', he writes, 'is often a healing blessing. Even the routine of providing for physical necessities may serve, like a fly-wheel, to carry people past a dead centre and on their way again. "Blessed be drudgery." During the first days of the bereavement crisis, the ceremonials, visitations and symbolisms of the funeral period serve to keep the bereaved family busy. In fact, many customs which to the unbereaved or "sophisticated" observer may seem useless, conventional, irrational, outworn or even superstitious may have certain values as evidence of affection and as distractions. Ceremonials have always been recognized as effective in the channelling and release or relaxation of the tensions to be dealt with in crises, quite apart from belief in immortality. Sincere rites may have profound psychological effects, either disturbing or comforting.'

In 1961 Dr. G. Engel published an article entitled *Is Grief a Disease?* in which he gives another definition of normal mourning:

'Generally it includes an initial phase of shock and disbelief, in which the sufferer attempts to deny the loss and to insulate himself against the shock of the reality. This is followed by a stage of developing awareness of the loss, marked by the painful effects of sadness, guilt, shame, helplessness or hopelessness; by a sense of loss and emptiness, by anorexia, sleep disturbances, sometimes somatic symptoms of pain or other discomfort, loss of interest in one's usual activities and associates; impairment of work performance etc. Finally there is a prolonged phase of restitution and recovery during which the work of mourning is carried on, the trauma of the loss is overcome, and a state of health and well-being re-established.'

In *Widows and Their Families*, published in 1956, Mr. Peter Marris analysed interviews with seventy-two working-class widows from three boroughs in London's East End, most of these widows being mothers of dependent children. His first two chapters on Grief and Mourning broke new ground in British social studies. After giving a number of telling quotations from his interviews he writes:

'All these signs of grief can be summarized as, first, physical symptoms; second, loss of contact with reality—inability to comprehend the loss, brooding over memories and clinging to possessions, a feeling that the dead man is still present, expecting him home with every turn of the key in the door and talking to him and of him as if he were still alive; third, a tendency to withdraw—to escape from everything that recalls the loss, from sympathetic friends and relatives, from any interest in life at all; fourth, hostility—against the doctor, against fate, inturned against oneself.'

Mr. Marris dealt exclusively with one aspect of bereavement, and all his mourners come from a single urban area; but in most respects his data and mine are strictly comparable.

Much the most thoroughgoing and elaborate investigation of the psychological components of grief and mourning is that on which Dr. John Bowlby is engaged; in May, 1964, he had published two of a projected series of five papers, *Grief and Mourning in Infancy and Early Childhood* (1960) and *Processes of Mourning* (1961). These two papers include a most complete study of the previous literature and exhaustive bibliographies. Dr. Bowlby's predominant interest is in the responses of infants and young children; he does not report any personal observations on adult mourners and relies almost exclusively on the descriptions of Lindemann and Marris, whose work, however, he in part reinterprets.

In *Processes of Mourning* he writes:

'In old and young, human and sub-human, loss of a loved object leads to a behavioural sequence which, varied though it be, is in some degree predictable. In human beings, moreover, the behavioural sequence is accompanied by a sequence of subjective experiences which begins with anxiety and anger, proceeds through pain and despair, and, if fortune smiles, ends with hope.'

His theory of mourning

'differentiates three main phases of mourning. Taking as the point of departure the hypothesis that the individual's attachment to his loved object is to be understood as mediated by a number of instinctual response systems, the first phase is seen as one during which the systems are still focussed on the original object but, because of the object's absence, whenever activated cannot be terminated. As a result the bereaved individual experiences repeated disappointment, persistent separation anxiety, and in so far as he suspects the worst, grief. This, however, is not all. So long as the response systems are focussed on the lost object there are strenuous and often angry efforts to recover it; and these efforts may continue despite their fruitlessness being painfully evident to others, and sometimes also to the bereaved himself. In this phase are sown, I believe, the seeds of much psychopathology. When the mourning process proceeds healthily, however, the response systems gradually cease to be focussed on the lost object and the efforts to recover it cease too. Disorganization of personality accompanied by pain and despair is the result. This is the second phase. The third phase completes the work of mourning and leads to a new and different state; during it a reorganization takes place, partly in connexion with the image of the lost object, partly in connexion with a new object or objects.'

In *Grief and Mourning in Infancy and Early Childhood* Dr. Bowlby groups the psychological responses of mourning under five main heads: (*a*) thought and behaviour still directed towards the lost object; (*b*) hostility, to whomsoever directed; (*c*) appeals for help; (*d*) despair, withdrawal, regression and disorganization; (*e*) reorganization of behaviour directed towards a new object.

As can be seen, there is a fairly general consensus among these writers of varying viewpoints and drawing their experience from a number of different societies, that there are three phases in normal mourning: a short period of shock, a period of intense grief, and a period of recovery and the resumption of normal social life; pathological mourning occurs when, for any reason, the third stage is not reached. To adapt Dr. Lindemann's statement, this may occur because the mourner avoids or postpones the painfulness of the second stage of intense grief, or because one or more of the components of the second stage are so distorted that it or they become either temporarily or permanently irreversible. The responses which I called 'hiding grief by busy-ness', 'mummification' and 'despair' fit adequately into Dr. Lindemann's categories of pathological mourning.

Mrs. Klein, Drs. Lindemann and Engel all state that guilt is an inevitable component of mourning; Messrs. Lindemann, Bowlby and Marris state that anger is an inevitable component. Although on theoretical grounds it seems probable that both these emotions are present on occasion, both guilt and anger are very inadequately illustrated in my interviews. A few of my informants (e.g. 1, 2, 32) indulged in some self-questioning; a few were bitter about the neglect with which they felt that they had been treated by the clergy, the deceased's former employer and the like; but both of these responses were exceptional. There are two possible explanations for this. The deaths which many of my respondents were mourning were natural deaths in the fullness of time; most of Dr. Lindemann's mourners were bereaved through the war or the disaster of the Cocoanut Grove fire; and Mr. Marris's widows were selected from those whose husbands had been fifty years old or under at death (*op. cit.*, p. 4). It is theoretically possible that the grief for a death which is considered 'natural' lacks some of the components of the grief felt when the death is premature, and is considered 'accidental', 'unfair', 'against the order of nature'. As I suggested (p. 121), the grief of a parent for a grown child seems to be of a different nature to the grief of an adult child for his parents, or of adults for spouses and siblings who have reached at least the beginnings of old age. The model of mourning in the existing scanty literature is very heavily biased towards premature and unexpected bereavement; it is possible that the lack of preparedness when death is due either to disaster or to a fatal heart-attack without previous warning may conduce to self-reproaches and to diffuse anger; and that these components are muted or absent when death is psychologically prepared for by nursing the dying person through his terminal illness, or at least being aware that the death is inevitable.[4]

It is also possible that the bereaved whom I interviewed had in fact felt guilt and expressed anger, but had not admitted to these disapproved-of emotions in the single interviews which I had with them. I was aware of the theoretical statements and was alert to any references to guilt or anger; the interviews were unstructured and my informants had the opportunity to express their feelings in any way which seemed good to them. Although most of them spoke with considerable frankness, there was also naturally some reticence; consequently I do not feel able to state categorically that guilt and anger are not inevitable components of the grief felt for a death 'in the course of nature'. I consider that further investigation is necessary before generalizations may be safely made.

[4] Dr. Samuel R. Lehrman writes in his article 'Reactions to Untimely Death' (*Psychiatric Quarterly*, 1956): 'Grief reactions are actually much more normal when death occurs in an aged person and has been expected. Under such circumstances, the work of mourning is done quickly, because a certain amount of this work . . . has already preceded the event of death. Pathological reactions to death are more frequent when the death is untimely and sudden.'
His article describes five cases of pathological mourning in response to an untimely death; there is no description of the 'more normal' grief reactions to which he refers.

Mr. Marris is the only writer of those quoted who is in any way concerned with the social life of mourners; indeed his major investigations concerned the contacts of the widow with her own and her husband's families, and the financial difficulties under which British widows with dependent children labour. All the other investigators tend to write as though the bereaved were completely alone, with no other occupation in life but to come to terms with and work through their grief. This is particularly marked in Dr. Lindemann's pioneering paper. His mourners were, it would seem, all studied in hospital where patients are typically alone with their ailments. When he writes of mourners who 'refuse visits lest they should precipitate the reaction [of intense grief]' (p. 142) he is almost certainly referring only to visitors to the hospital, and not to callers at the home. Since Dr. Lindemann's paper has been so influential, this implicit picture of the solitary patient who has nothing to do but get over his grief has tended to dominate the literature of the last twenty years.

With the exception of hospitalized patients, and occasional widows or widowers who are childless or whose children are widely dispersed, this picture of the solitary mourner alone with his grief would seem to be a very considerable simplification. Grief is, of course, an endopsychic experience and the working through of mourning is psychological; but it is my contention that the work of mourning can be assisted or impeded, and its benign outcome facilitated or rendered more difficult by the way in which the mourner is treated by his society in general and, in particular, those members of it with whom he is in frequent contact, including members of his own family. The only explicit recognition of the role which society can play in assisting mourning that I have found in the literature is the paragraph by Mrs. Klein (quoted on p. 140) in which she states that if the mourner has people whom he loves and who share his grief, and if he can accept their sympathy, the benign work of mourning will be promoted. Dr. Bowlby included among the psychological responses of mourning 'appeals for help' (p. 147); but to date he has not elaborated this single statement in any way, as far as adults are concerned, though he stresses that crying is very frequently an infantile appeal for help; the crying of adults implicitly carries a similar connotation. It is my contention that adults *need* help in living through the phase of intense grief; but I question whether they can appeal for help at all explicitly in a society, such as contemporary Britain, where the majority wish to ignore grief and treat mourning as morbid.

Similarly, the aid which ritual may give in dealing with grief and providing patterns for mourning is almost completely ignored. The relevant paragraph by Dr. Eliot is quoted on p. 144; Peter Marris has two pages (*op. cit.*, pp. 31–2) in which he refers to some of the rites of the Trobrianders, Tallensi and Azande; and in *The Meaning of Death* (edited by Dr. Herman Feifel), Dr. David G. Mandelbaum contributed a chapter entitled 'Social Uses of Funeral Rites'.[5] He opens his discussion with the statement that 'rites performed for the dead have important effects for the living'; and he illustrates this with a detailed study of the funeral rites of the Kota of South India, and briefer examinations of the rites of three American Indian tribes, the Hebridean island of Barra and a town in Java to demonstrate that 'funeral rites are generally intended to be a means of strengthening group solidarity'. 'American culture', he writes,

'has, in certain respects, and for some Americans, become deritualized. Persons bereaved by a death sometimes find that they have no clear prescription as to what to do next. In such cases each has to work out a solution for himself. After the typical period of shock and disorganization, these mourners can receive little help towards personal reorganization.'

My material demonstrates that this generalization is equally applicable to the majority of those bereaved in Britain.

[5] *Op. cit.*, pp. 189–217.

To sum up, my material confirms the statement that mourning typically falls into three stages, an initial period of shock, a stage of violent grief and disorganization and a usually longer period of reorganization, and advances the hypothesis that the median duration of the second stage is between six and twelve weeks, in Britain. Since my interviews were not primarily psychiatrically oriented, I cannot contribute to the analysis of the components of grief or the discussion of the psychological mechanisms involved in mourning, except to raise the question whether either guilt or anger are inevitable components in every type of bereavement. Finally, I call attention to the potentially important roles played by ritual and by those members of society with whom the mourner comes in contact in giving help to the mourner in the period of shock and the stage of violent grief and assisting him in giving expression to and working through his distress; and to the maladaptations which may result if this help is not forthcoming. This aspect of mourning has barely been touched on by previous writers.

QUESTIONNAIRE AND STATISTICAL TABLES

The Questionnaire

Q. 1a. Have you ever attended a funeral or cremation? — Yes. No.

1b. How long ago was the last time you attended a funeral or cremation? — Less than a year ago; more than 1 year but less than 3 years. 3 years up to and including 5 years. Over 5 years.

IF WITHIN THE LAST FIVE YEARS—
1c. Who was it for? — Close relative: Parent, spouse, sibling, child. Secondary relative: Grandparent, grandchild, uncle/aunt, cousin or other blood-relation, in-law. Not related.

1d. IF SECONDARY OR OTHER—Apart from that one, have you attended the funeral of any member of your immediate family during the past five years? Immediate family means parents, brothers or sisters, spouse or children. — Yes. No.

1e. If 'Yes', would you tell me who that was? — Parent, spouse, sibling, child.

Q. 2a. Would you object to answering a few more questions about your bereavement? — Yes. No.

2b. What type of denominational service was the funeral of your ——? — Jewish. C. of E. C. of Scotland. Baptist. Congregational.

Methodist.
Roman Catholic.
Non-denominational.
'Christian.'
Other (state).

2c. Did you wear
anything you would
not normally wear at
other times?

Armband, tie.
Major apparel.
Nothing.

2d. Did you wear
mourning after the
day of the funeral?

Yes. No.

2e. If YES, for how long
did you wear it?

Less than a week.
A month or less.
3 months or less.
Over 3 months.
Can't remember.

Q. 3a. Before the funeral,
did the family gather
at the house?

Yes. No.

3b. Before the funeral,
were there any
ceremonies at the
house involving
prayers or anything
like that, with or
without a priest?

Yes. No.

3c. Were there any
signs that this was a
house of mourning,
such as drawn blinds,
mourning cards, etc.?

Drawn blinds.
Mourning cards.
Other (state).
No signs.

3d. Were there any
ceremonies or family
gatherings *after* the
funeral?

Yes. No.

3e. Were there any
special visits of
condolence or offers
of help from
neighbours or
relatives?

Yes, neighbours.
Yes, relatives.
No.

Q. 4a. Were there any
leisure activities that
you gave up for a
time after the
funeral?

Yes. No.

4b. If YES, what were they? For how long did you give them up?

Q. 5a. Would you describe yourself as being of any denomination?

Yes. No.

5b. If YES, which one?

Jewish.
C. of E.
C. of Scotland.
Baptist.
Congregational.
Methodist.
Roman Catholic.
'Christian.'
Other (state).

5c. How often do you normally attend a church service?

More than once a week.
Weekly.
Less than once a week, but up to and including once a month.
Less than once a month.
Special occasions only.
Never.

5d. Do you ever say any private prayers? How often?

More than once a day.
Daily.
Less frequently.
Only on special occasions.
Never.

5e. Do you believe in the Devil?

Yes. No. Don't know.

5f. Do you believe in an afterlife?

Yes. No. Uncertain.

5g. If YES, what will it be like?

Q. 6a. Where did —— die?

Hospital.
Home.
Elsewhere.

6b. Were you present when he (she) died?

Yes. No.

6c. Did you pay your respects to the body before the funeral?

Yes. No.

6d. If NO, have you ever
seen the body of
someone who has
died from natural
causes?

Yes. No.

Q. 7a. Do you think you
saw more or less of
your friends after
you were bereaved?

More. Less. Same.

7b. Do you think you
gained weight, lost
weight or stayed the
same?

Gained. Lost. Same.

7c. How did you sleep?

Same. Less well. Better.

7d. Had you any
children under 16
years then?

Yes. No.

7e. If YES, what did you
tell them about
death?

7f. Is this more or less
what you were told
when you were
young?

7g. If NO, in what way
was it different?

Q. 8. Would you be
willing to allow
somebody to come
and talk to you about
your experiences
since your
bereavement?

Yes. No.

Notes on the Tables
The answers to every question were analysed by sex, age, social class, region, town size, marital status, relation to the informant, religion of the informant. I am reproducing full tables of the answers to Questions 3 (*a*) (*b*) (*c*); 6 (*a*) (*b*) (*c*) (*d*) and 7 (*a*) (*b*) (*c*). For the remainder of the questions, I am only reproducing those breakdowns which seem to be significant; and I am not reproducing the tables on the answers to Questions 4 (*b*), 7 (*d*), 7 (*e*) as the numbers are too few and the scatter too great for the tables to carry much significance. The answers to Question 5 are considered in Appendix Three, where they are compared to answers given to the same questions in 1950; and the answers to Question 8 are considered later on in this Appendix when I discuss how I selected the people for re-interviewing.

TABLE I
ATTENDANCE AT FUNERAL OR CREMATION (Question 1a)
All contacts
(by Sex, Age, Social Grade and Region)

	Total		Sex				Age						
			Male		Female		16-34		35-44		45-54		55+
All contacts (base for percentages)	1628		762		866		535		299		303		491
	No.	%	No.	%	No.	%	No.	%	No.	%	No.	%	No.	%
LAST ATTENDED FUNERAL/CREMATION:														
Less than 1 year ago	361	22	197	26	164	19	77	14	72	24	85	28	127	26
1 year but less than 3 years	349	21	158	21	191	22	97	18	63	21	90	30	99	20
3 years up to and including 5 years	193	12	91	12	102	12	58	11	43	14	37	12	55	11
Over 5 years	479	30	207	27	272	31	113	21	93	31	81	27	192	39
Never attended, or no answer	246	15	109	14	137	16	190	36	28	10	10	3	18	4
TOTAL	1628	100	762	100	866	100	535	100	299	100	303	100	491	100
IN LAST 5 YEARS ATTENDED FUNERAL/ CREMATION FOR:														
Close relatives:														
Parent	197	12	96	13	101	12	48	9	52	17	68	22	29	6
Spouse	67	4	23	3	44	5	1	*	2	1	17	6	47	10
Sibling	87	5	37	5	50	6	6	1	5	2	21	7	55	11
Child	15	1	9	1	6	1	2	*	6	2	1	*	6	1
Other person only	537	33	281	37	256	29	175	33	113	38	105	35	144	29
Not attended	725	45	316	41	409	47	303	57	121	40	91	30	210	43
TOTAL	1628	100	762	100	866	100	535	100	299	100	303	100	491	100

TABLE I—continued
ATTENDANCE AT FUNERAL OR CREMATION (Question 1a)
All contacts
(by Sex, Age, Social Grade and Region)

All contacts (base for percentages)	Social Grade								Region											
	AB 221		C1 266		C2 583		DE 558		South, East, S.-East 546		Wales and S.-West 216		Midlands and N. Midlands 267		North-West 203		North 244		Scotland 152	
	No.	%	No.	%	No.	%	No.	%	No.	%	No.	%	No.	%	No.	%	No.	%	No.	%
LAST ATTENDED FUNERAL/CREMATION:																				
Less than 1 year ago	61	28	63	24	126	22	111	20	108	20	48	22	54	20	31	15	60	25	60	39
1 year but less than 3 years	55	25	56	21	129	22	109	20	86	16	63	29	61	23	51	25	52	21	36	24
3 years up to and including 5 years	27	12	43	16	62	11	61	11	65	12	26	12	29	11	27	14	33	14	13	9
Over 5 years	53	24	63	24	165	28	198	35	188	34	45	21	76	28	73	36	69	28	28	18
Never attended, or no answer	25	11	41	15	101	17	79	14	99	18	34	16	47	18	21	10	30	12	15	10
TOTAL	221	100	266	100	583	100	558	100	546	100	216	100	267	100	203	100	244	100	152	100
IN LAST 5 YEARS ATTENDED FUNERAL/CREMATION FOR:																				
Close relative:																				
Parent	27	12	34	13	82	14	54	10	58	11	27	13	37	14	21	10	29	12	25	16
Spouse	7	3	14	5	9	1	37	7	16	3	12	6	8	3	6	3	11	5	14	9
Sibling	13	6	6	2	27	5	41	7	24	4	12	6	17	6	15	8	12	5	7	5
Child	2	1	2	1	3	1	8	1	5	1	1	*	4	2	2	1	1	1	1	1
Other person only	94	43	106	40	196	34	141	25	156	29	85	39	78	29	65	32	91	37	62	41
Not attended	78	35	104	39	266	45	277	50	287	52	79	36	123	46	94	46	99	40	43	28
TOTAL	221	100	266	100	583	100	558	100	546	100	216	100	267	100	203	100	244	100	152	100

TABLE II

IF YOU ATTENDED A FUNERAL OR CREMATION IN THE LAST
FIVE YEARS, WHO WAS IT FOR? (*Question 1c*)

	Number	Percentage
Close relative only:		
Parent	154	17
Spouse	55	6
Sibling	67	7
Child	14	2
Secondary relative:		
Grandparent	67	7
Grandchild	1	—
Uncle/Aunt	87	10
Cousin or other blood relation	32	4
In-law	186	21
Other person not related	240	26
TOTAL	903	100
Close relative in addition to secondary relative or other person		
Parent	43	5
Spouse	12	1
Sibling	20	2
Child	1	—

(NOTE: Out of the 366 people who had lost a primary relative, 7 were unwilling to answer further questions about their bereavement.)

TABLE III

WHAT TYPE OF DENOMINATIONAL SERVICE WAS THE FUNERAL OR CREMATION OF YOUR ——? (*Question 2b*)

Type of service	Total	16–34	35–44	45–54	55+
Jewish	1	—	2	—	1
C. of E.	68	63	64	70	71
Church of Scotland	9	17	5	8	8
Baptist	1	—	—	1	1
Congregational	1	—	—	4	1
Methodist	6	5	7	7	5
Roman Catholic	9	9	15	8	7
Nondenominational	1	—	2	—	1
Other and Don't know	4	6	2	2	3

TABLE IV (BY REGION)

	South-East	South-West	Mid-lands	North-West	North-East	Scot-land
Jewish	1	—	—	—	2	—
Church of England	82	79	76	62	74	15
Church of Scotland	—	—	—	2	2	65
Baptist	1	4	—	—	—	—
Congregational	1	2	—	2	—	5
Methodist	5	11	6	10	5	—
Roman Catholic	5	4	6	24	10	13
Nondenominational	—	—	2	—	2	—
Other and Don't know	5	—	10	—	4	2

TABLE V

DID YOU WEAR ANYTHING FOR MOURNING THAT YOU WOULD
NOT NORMALLY WEAR AT OTHER TIMES? IF YOU WORE
MOURNING AFTER THE DAY OF THE FUNERAL, FOR HOW LONG
DID YOU WEAR IT? (*Questions 2c, d, e*)

	Total	Male	Female
Armband, tie	33	66	5
Major apparel	33	21	44
Nothing	37	20	52
TOTAL	103	107	101
Less than a week	5	8	2
A month or less	15	21	9
3 months or less	11	12	11
Over 3 months	20	18	22
Can't remember	2	1	3
Did not wear mourning and not answered	47	40	53

TABLE VI (BY AGE)

	16–34	35–44	45–54	Over 55
Armband, tie	41	33	30	32
Major apparel	35	36	32	32
Nothing	31	36	39	39
TOTAL	107	105	101	103
Less than a week	11	5	3	4
A month or less	29	19	9	12
3 months or less	6	14	13	10
Over 3 months	6	6	28	27
Can't remember	—	3	—	4
Did not wear mourning and not answered	48	53	47	43

TABLE VII (BY SOCIAL GRADE)

	AB	C1	C2	DE
Armband, tie	40	31	38	27
Major apparel	19	33	29	42
Nothing	44	42	34	36
TOTAL	103	106	101	105
Less than a week	4	4	5	6
A month or less	19	9	18	13
3 months or less	13	13	13	8
Over 3 months	8	20	15	29
Can't remember	—	2	1	4
Did not wear mourning and not answered	56	52	48	40

TABLE VIII (BY REGION)

	South-East	South-West	Mid-lands	North-West	North-East	Scot-land
Armband, tie	35	35	24	19	39	43
Major apparel	34	21	34	45	31	35
Nothing	34	44	42	36	39	30
TOTAL	103	100	100	100	109	108
Less than a week	6	—	10	2	4	6
A month or less	17	12	13	10	13	22
3 months or less	17	6	13	7	7	9
Over 3 months	17	13	22	31	26	15
Can't remember	2	4	2	2	—	2
Did not wear mourning and not answered	41	65	40	48	50	46

TABLE IX (BY RELATIVE MOURNED)

(NOTE: Absolute figures are given for a child, percentages for others.)

	Parent	Spouse	Sibling	Child
Armband, tie	36	24	31	(5)
Major apparel	32	45	24	(6)
Nothing	35	33	48	(4)
TOTAL	103	102	103	(15)
Less than a week	4	3	7	(2)
A month or less	18	11	13	(1)
3 months or less	14	12	5	(1)
Over 3 months	12	42	19	(5)
Can't remember	2	3	2	—
Did not wear mourning and not answered	50	29	54	(6)

TABLE X

BEFORE THE FUNERAL, DID THE FAMILY GATHER AT THE HOUSE? BEFORE THE FUNERAL WERE THERE ANY CEREMONIES AT THE HOUSE, INVOLVING PRAYERS OR ANYTHING LIKE THAT, WITH OR WITHOUT A PRIEST? WERE THERE ANY SIGNS THAT THIS WAS A HOUSE OF MOURNING, SUCH AS DRAWN BLINDS, MOURNING CARDS, ETC.? (Questions 3a, b, c)

	Total	Male	Female
Family gatherings:			
Yes	82	82	82
No	18	18	18
Ceremonies in home:			
Yes	24	27	22
No	76	73	78

Drawn blinds	76	73	78
Mourning cards	15	18	13
Other signs	2	2	1
No signs	20	24	17
TOTAL	113	117	109

TABLE XI (BY AGE)

	16–34	35–44	45–54	Over 55
Family gatherings:				
Yes	83	83	84	80
No	17	17	16	20
Ceremonies in home:				
Yes	35	28	24	18
No	65	72	76	82
Drawn blinds	72	72	75	79
Mourning cards	19	17	17	12
Other signs	—	3	1	2
No signs	24	20	22	18
TOTAL	115	112	115	111

TABLE XII (BY REGION)

	South-East	South-West	Mid-lands	North-West	North-East	Scot-land
Family gatherings:						
Yes	84	79	87	79	85	74
No	16	21	13	21	15	26
Ceremonies in home:						
Yes	9	21	23	21	26	63
No	91	79	77	79	74	37
Drawn blinds	63	73	85	93	87	65
Mourning cards	11	6	15	24	2	46
Other signs	1	2	2	—	—	4
No signs	31	25	11	7	13	24
TOTAL	106	106	113	124	102	139

TABLE XIII (BY SOCIAL GRADE)

	AB	C1	C2	DE
Family gatherings:				
Yes	71	82	86	83
No	29	18	14	17
Ceremonies in home:				
Yes	19	22	21	29
No	81	78	79	71
Drawn blinds	67	69	78	80
Mourning cards	10	20	17	14
Other signs	2	—	2	1
No signs	29	27	18	17
TOTAL	108	118	115	112

TABLE XIV (BY TOWN SIZE)

	Under 50,000	50,000–100,000	100,000–250,000	Over 250,000
Family gatherings:				
Yes	82	85	78	86
No	18	15	22	14
Ceremonies in home:				
Yes	29	16	22	33
No	71	84	78	67
Drawn blinds	78	72	75	81
Mourning cards	23	7	17	12
Other signs	1	2	—	2
No signs	18	25	20	17
TOTAL	120	106	112	112

TABLE XV (BY MARITAL STATUS)

	Married	Widowed	Single or divorced
Family gatherings:			
Yes	83	76	93
No	17	24	7
Ceremonies in home:			
Yes	23	21	33
No	77	79	67
Drawn blinds	75	83	67
Mourning cards	14	17	16
Other signs	2	1	—
No signs	22	13	26
TOTAL	113	114	109

TABLE XVI (BY RELATIVE MOURNED)

(NOTE: Absolute figures are given for a child, percentages for others.)

	Parent	Spouse	Sibling	Child
Family gatherings:				
Yes	85	76	83	(10)
No	15	24	17	(5)
Ceremonies in home:				
Yes	26	24	16	(7)
No	74	76	84	(8)
Drawn blinds	71	80	85	(10)
Mourning cards	15	21	10	(4)
Other signs	2	4	—	—
No signs	24	15	14	(4)
TOTAL	112	120	109	(18)

TABLE XVII (BY RELIGION OF INFORMANT)

(NOTE: This table is in absolute figures, not in percentages. Under 'Church of Scotland, etc.' are included Baptists, Congregationalists and Methodists.)

	Church of England	Roman Catholic	Church of Scotland, etc.	Jewish/ other	None
Family gatherings:					
Yes	188	31	54	6	16
No	34	8	13	2	7
Ceremonies in home:					
Yes	31	18	32	1	4
No	191	21	35	7	19
Drawn blinds	174	32	48	3	15
Mourning cards	21	11	18	—	5
Other signs	2	1	2	—	—
No signs	41	5	15	5	7
TOTAL	222	39	67	8	23

TABLE XVIII

WERE THERE ANY CEREMONIES OR FAMILY GATHERINGS AFTER FUNERAL? WERE THERE SPECIAL VISITS OF CONDOLENCE OR OFFERS OF HELP FROM NEIGHBOURS OR RELATIVES? (*Question 3d, e*)

(BY AGE)

	16–34	35–44	45–54	Over 55
Ceremonies/gatherings after funerals:				
Yes	83	72	74	76
No	17	28	26	24

Special visits:				
Neighbours	80	69	61	64
Relatives	69	56	58	60
None	17	22	26	24
Not answered	—	—	1	1
TOTAL	166	147	146	149

TABLE XIX (BY REGION)

	South-East	South-West	Mid-lands	North-West	North-East	Scot-land
Ceremonies/ gatherings after funeral:						
Yes	70	48	85	76	89	91
No	30	52	15	24	11	9
Special visits:						
Neighbours	60	58	68	60	76	83
Relatives	47	58	61	50	74	85
None	28	25	24	31	15	11
Not answered	1	2	2	—	—	—
TOTAL	136	143	155	141	165	179

TABLE XX

WERE THERE ANY LEISURE ACTIVITIES THAT YOU GAVE UP FOR A TIME AFTER THE FUNERAL? (*Question 4a*)

	Total	Male	Female
Yes	18	21	16
No	82	79	84

TABLE XXI (BY AGE)

	16–34	35–44	45–54	Over 55
Yes	33	23	19	10
No	67	77	81	90

TABLE XXII (BY RELATIVE MOURNED)

(NOTE: Absolute figures are given for a child; percentages for others.)

	Parent	Spouse	Sibling	Child
Yes	21	21	9	(3)
No	79	79	91	(12)

TABLE XXIII

WHERE DID —— DIE? WERE YOU PRESENT WHEN HE (SHE) DIED? DID YOU PAY YOUR RESPECTS TO THE BODY BEFORE THE FUNERAL? IF NO, HAVE YOU EVER SEEN THE BODY OF SOMEONE WHO HAS DIED OF NATURAL CAUSES? (*Question 6a, b, c, d*)

	Total	Male	Female
Died in hospital	50	51	50
at home	44	43	44
elsewhere	6	6	6
Not answered	*	—	*
Present:			
Yes	24	18	29
No	76	82	71
Not answered	*	—	*
Paid respects to body	69	73	65
Did not, but have seen body	24	22	26
Have not seen body	6	4	8
No answer	1	1	1

(NOTE: One woman refused to answer where her sibling had died; and two men and three women refused to say whether they had ever seen the body of someone who had died of natural causes. These respondents' replies will be omitted in the following analyses to the replies to these questions. * = less than .5%.)

TABLE XXIV (BY AGE)

	16–34	35–44	45–54	Over 55
Died in hospital	52	56	49	48
at home	41	36	44	48
elsewhere	7	8	7	3
Present at death:				
Yes	28	16	25	26
No	72	84	75	73
Paid respects to body	68	63	68	72
Did not, but have seen body	15	23	28	25
Have not seen dead body	15	9	3	3

TABLE XXV (BY SOCIAL GRADE)

	AB	C1	C2	DE
Died in hospital	56	45	54	47
at home	40	51	39	46
elsewhere	4	4	6	7
Present at death:				
Yes	12	22	24	28
No	88	78	75	72
Paid respects to body	48	68	67	77
Did not, but have seen body	42	22	25	18
Have not seen dead body	6	5	8	5

TABLE XXVI (BY REGION)

	South-East	South-West	Mid-lands	North-West	North-East	Scotland
Died in hospital	48	50	42	50	52	65
at home	46	42	55	45	43	26
elsewhere	6	8	3	5	5	7
Present at death:						
Yes	21	29	18	26	24	31
No	79	71	82	74	76	67
Paid respects to body	65	61	56	95	74	70
Did not, but have seen body	29	33	29	5	14	26
Have not seen dead body	5	6	15	—	6	2

TABLE XXVII (BY TOWN SIZE)

	Under 50,000	50,000–100,000	100,000–250,000	Over 250,000
Died in hospital	53	47	49	52
at home	39	50	44	43
elsewhere	7	3	7	5
Present at death:				
Yes	25	18	28	26
No	74	82	72	74
Paid respects to body	67	63	76	69
Did not, but have seen body	25	31	18	17
Have not seen dead body	7	6	1	14

TABLE XXVIII (BY MARITAL STATUS)

	Married	Widowed	Single or divorced
Died in hospital	50	49	54
at home	43	46	44
elsewhere	7	5	2
Present at death:			
Yes	16	43	30
No	84	57	70
Paid respects to body	66	78	60
Did not, but have seen			
dead body	26	20	26
Have not seen dead body	6	2	14

TABLE XXIX (BY RELATIVE MOURNED)

(NOTE: Absolute figures are given for a child; percentages for others.)

	Parent	Spouse	Sibling	Child
Died in hospital	48	50	52	(11)
at home	48	42	41	(1)
elsewhere	4	8	6	(3)
Present at death:				
Yes	24	47	7	(2)
No	76	53	92	(13)
Paid respects to body	67	77	63	(12)
Did not, but have seen body	23	21	29	(3)
Have not seen dead body	7	2	8	—

TABLE XXX (BY RELIGION OF INFORMANT)

(NOTE: This table is in absolute figures, not in percentages.)

	C. of E.	R.C.	Church of Scotland, etc.	Jewish and other	None
Died in hospital	105	24	37	4	11
at home	105	12	26	4	10
elsewhere	12	3	3	—	2
Present at death:					
Yes	54	12	13	1	6
No	168	27	53	7	17
Paid respects to body	151	33	45	3	14
Did not, but have seen body	53	6	19	3	6
Have not seen dead body	15	—	2	2	2
TOTAL	222	39	67	8	23

TABLE XXXI

DO YOU THINK YOU SAW MORE OR LESS OF YOUR FRIENDS AFTER YOU WERE BEREAVED? DO YOU THINK YOU GAINED WEIGHT, LOST WEIGHT OR STAYED THE SAME? HOW DID YOU SLEEP? (*Question 7a, b, c*)

(NOTE: One woman refused to answer any of these questions; one man did not answer the question on weight. They are omitted from the following tabulations.)

	Total	Male	Female
Saw friends more	20	17	22
less	15	15	16
the same	65	68	61

Weight gained	4	5	4
lost	36	24	46
same	59	70	49
Slept same	42	58	29
less well	55	41	67
better	3	1	3

TABLE XXXII (BY AGE)

	16–34	35–44	45–54	Over 55
Saw friends more	17	17	20	23
less	28	20	7	15
the same	55	63	73	61
Weight gained	—	3	6	6
lost	41	41	32	35
the same	59	56	62	57
Slept same	35	37	47	44
less well	65	58	51	52
better	—	5	2	3

TABLE XXXIII (BY SOCIAL GRADE)

	AB	C1	C2	DE
Saw friends more	17	20	13	28
less	8	16	14	18
the same	75	64	72	54
Weight gained	2	2	7	4
lost	27	56	28	39
the same	69	42	64	57
Slept same	54	36	45	38
less well	38	64	51	61
better	8	—	3	1

TABLE XXXIV (BY REGION)

	South-East	South-West	Mid-lands	North-West	North-East	Scot-land
Saw friends more	17	27	13	17	18	33
less	16	11	21	12	17	13
the same	67	62	66	71	65	52
Weight gained	7	6	5	2	4	—
lost	27	31	40	43	48	39
the same	68	63	55	55	48	59
Slept same	44	63	34	57	37	20
less well	53	33	63	43	59	78
better	3	4	3	—	4	—

TABLE XXXV (BY TOWN SIZE)

	Under 50,000	50,000– 100,000	100,000– 250,000	Over 250,000
Saw friends more	23	17	20	19
less	9	19	14	29
the same	67	64	66	52
Weight gained	3	8	2	5
lost	40	25	42	40
the same	56	66	56	55
Slept same	40	48	43	33
less well	56	50	55	64
better	3	2	2	2

TABLE XXXVI (BY MARITAL STATUS)

	Married	Widowed	Single or divorced
Saw friends more	13	37	23
less	12	20	23
the same	74	43	54
Weight gained	4	5	5
lost	30	57	26
the same	65	38	67
Slept same	47	28	49
less well	51	67	49
better	2	5	2

TABLE XXXVII (BY RELATIVE MOURNED)

(NOTE: Absolute figures are given for a child; percentages for others.)

	Parent	Spouse	Sibling	Child
Saw friends more	16	44	9	(4)
less	16	18	12	(3)
the same	68	38	78	(8)
Weight gained	5	3	6	—
lost	32	71	16	(8)
the same	63	26	77	(7)
Slept same	47	17	57	(2)
less well	50	80	41	(12)
better	3	3	1	(1)

TABLE XXXVIII (BY RELIGION OF INFORMANT)

(NOTE: This table is in absolute figures, not in percentages.)

	C. of E.	R.C.	Church of Scotland, etc.	Jewish etc.	None
Saw friends more	37	10	21	2	2
less	34	7	6	2	6
the same	151	22	39	4	15
Weight gained	14	—	1	—	1
lost	72	13	35	3	7
the same	135	26	30	5	15
Slept same	96	16	26	4	10
less well	119	22	39	4	13
better	7	1	1	—	—

Sampling areas

The following is a list of the sampling areas by regions in which the interviewers asked their questions. The areas in italics are those in which I conducted interviews.

South-East Region: *Beckenham*, Bognor, *Brighton*, Colchester, *Finchley*, Godalming, *Gravesend*, Hitchin, *Hove*, *Ipswich*, *Kensington*, Leatherhead, *Littlehampton*, Mitcham, *Orpington*, Sevenoaks, *Shoreham*, Southall, *St. Marylebone*, Sutton, *Wandsworth*, *Westminster*, Wimbledon, *Woolwich*, Worthing.

South-West Region: *Bath*, *Brixham*, Cardiff, Dawlish, *Exeter*, *Exmouth*, Gloucester, Haverfordwest, Paignton, *Torquay*.

Midland Region: *Birmingham*, *Cannock*, *Dudley*, Kettering, Northampton, *Smethwick*, Solihull, Wellingborough, *West Bromwich*, *Wolverhampton*.

North-East Region: *Gateshead*, Knaresborough, *Leeds*,

Middlesborough, Selby, *South Shields, Sunderland, Tyne-mouth*, Wallsend, *York.*

North-West Region: *Accrington, Blackburn, Blackpool,* Bury, *Lancaster*, Manchester, Morecambe and Heysham, *Preston.*

Scotland: *Arbroath, Carnoustie, Dundee*, Edinburgh, Glasgow, *Monifrieth.*

Selection of Informants for further interviewing

At the end of the questionnaire, all the respondents were asked, 'Would you be willing to allow somebody to come and talk to you at greater length about your experiences since your bereavement?' Those who refused were left a form letter which explained the object of the research which they could return if they changed their mind. Quite a few did so. Out of the 359 people who had answered the questionnaire, 212 were willing to grant a further interview, and 147 were not. These two groups can be analysed as follows (I am giving absolute figures, not percentages, as many of the numbers are small).

TABLE XXXIX

Sex	Agree to further interview	Do not agree
Male	108	56
Female	104	91
Age		
16–34	33	21
35–44	38	26
45–54	64	41
over 55	77	59

TABLE XXXIX (cont'd)

Social Class	Agree to further interview	Do not agree
AB	29	19
C1	33	22
C2	63	56
DE	87	50
Regions		
South-East	57	46
South-West	26	26
Midlands	39	23
North-West	23	19
North-East	35	19
Scotland	32	14
Town size		
under 50,000	68	54
50,000–100,000	66	40
100,000–250,000	56	33
over 250,000	22	20
Marital status		
married	132	98
widowed	56	30
single and divorced	24	19
Relative of informant who had died		
Parent	114	78
Spouse	45	21
Sibling	42	44
Child	11	4

As can be seen, there was a relatively marked unwillingness to talk about their bereavement on the part of women, the skilled working class, inhabitants of the two Southern regions, of the smallest and the largest towns, and those who had lost a brother or sister.

I thought there might be a correlation between the willingness to grant a further interview and the extent to which the informant had shown signs of mourning and disturbed social life, as measured by Questions 7a, b, c; my hypothesis was that those whose mourning had been acute would be more willing to talk about their experiences than those who had not been so distressed. The figures would seem to justify this expectation, in so far as those who lost weight and sleep have a high proportion of those willing to be interviewed; and those who gained weight and slept better are markedly unwilling to be interviewed; but the figures, particularly of the last-mentioned categories, are so small that not too much weight can be put on them.

TABLE XL

	Agree to further interview	Do not agree
Saw friends		
More	53	19
Less	32	23
The same	127	104
Weight		
Gained	5	11
Lost	80	50
The same	127	84
Slept		
The same	87	65
Less well	122	75
Better	3	6

(NOTE: The numbers do not quite add up to 359, as there were one or two people who did not answer any of these questions.)

Since I did not feel it would be practical for me to attempt to interview all 212 people who were willing to be interviewed, I divided this population into three categories, A, B, C, according to the relative who had been lost and the length of time since the bereavement had occurred. In Category A, I placed all who had lost children, those who had lost a brother or sister, husband or wife within three years, and those who had lost a parent within the year. I also moved into this category members of uncommon religious sects and people under 21, whatever the nature and time of their bereavement. Category B was made up of those who had lost a brother or sister, husband or wife, between 3 and 5 years previously, and those who had lost a parent between 1 and 3 years previously; Category C consisted of those who had lost a parent more than 3 years previously. I then sorted the questionnaires out according to their geographical sampling areas, and discarded all those areas which had respondents in category C exclusively. Any area which had two respondents in category A was marked for visiting, and all the respondents in that area were included. For the areas which had one or no category A respondent, and one or more category B respondents, the decision whether to include or exclude them was made on geographical grounds; if they were within approximately fifty miles of an area already selected for visiting they were included, otherwise no. This selection produced 114 names and addresses, approximately half of those who were willing to give a further interview, and a little under a third of the total sample.

In the result, I only secured eighty interviews. Eight men and six women had moved between the interviews in April and May and my visits in October and November; the new residents in their house or flats did not have a forwarding address. Two women had died, one had committed suicide and one man and one woman were in hospital. Two men and two women refused to give a further interview; and five men and six women could not be contacted despite repeated calls. These seemed to be lonely people, for their neighbours could say nothing about their movements; in two cases more than one day's supply of milk was standing outside the door.

Although I had wanted to interview young mourners, this turned out to be difficult to accomplish. On several occasions the surviving parent, typically the mother, was in the house when I called; whether the young son or daughter was present or no, she invariably took charge of the interview. I therefore have recorded rather more widows and rather fewer orphans than I had planned.

APPENDIX THREE

RELIGIOUS BELIEFS
AND PRACTICES
1963 and 1950 compared

Since Questions 5 *a, b, c, d, e, f, g,* in the present survey are the same as those asked in *Exploring English Character*[1] it seemed worth while comparing the patterns of the two surveys, even though the samples are not strictly comparable. The present survey consists of verbal answers given to interviewers by 359 people selected out of a stratified sample because of their recent bereavement, and including respondents from Scotland and Wales as well as England. The people whose replies were analysed in *Exploring English Character* were from England only, and consisted of 4,983 anonymous volunteers who had filled in a voluminous questionnaire in January, 1950. The fact that the questionnaires were anonymous may account for the greater proportion of people who

[1] Geoffrey Gorer: *Exploring English Character* (Cresset Press, 1955. Criterion Books, N.Y., 1955). Chapter XIV and (in the complete editions) Tables 82, 83, 84, 85, 90, 92, 93.

admitted to potentially disapproved-of beliefs and attitudes, such as denying adherence to any creed or religion; but the similarity of the patterns of responses, and in some cases, of the actual figures, makes it probable that these figures do represent current beliefs and attitudes in England. Since the criteria for social class (in this survey by the Registrar-General's classification of occupations, in *Exploring English Character* by self-ascription) are different in the two surveys, and town sizes are also grouped differently, I have not thought it useful to reproduce these analyses; sex and regions are constant and I have, except for Question 5g, given these breakdowns as well as the totals.

In this survey only 6 per cent disclaimed adherence to some religion or denomination, whereas in *Exploring English Character* 23 per cent gave this answer. The pattern of unbelief is as follows:

TABLE XLI

PERCENTAGE OF PEOPLE DISCLAIMING RELIGION OR DENOMINATION

	Present survey	'Exploring English Character'
Total percentage	6	23
Male	9	26
Female	4	18
Regions		
South-East	9	25
South-West	7	16
Midlands	11	24
North-West	—	17
North-East	2	24

TABLE XLII

PERCENTAGE OF PEOPLE CLAIMING ADHERENCE TO SOME
RELIGION OR DENOMINATION (*Question 5a*)

Creed	Present survey	'Exploring English Character'
Jewish	1	1
Church of England	61	59
Church of Scotland	8	—
Baptist	1	3
Congregational	2	3
Methodist	8	10
Roman Catholic	11	8
'Christian'	1	3
Other (Spiritualist, etc.)	2	5
Presbyterian, Nonconformist, Protestant	—	8

TABLE XLIII

DISTRIBUTION OF DENOMINATIONS BY REGION

(a) Present survey

Denomination	South-East	South-West	Mid-lands	North-West	North-East
Jewish	—	—	—	—	1
Church of England	77	64	74	50	60
Church of Scotland	—	—	—	2	2
Baptist	1	4	2	—	—
Congregational	1	4	—	2	—
Methodist	4	7	5	19	16
Roman Catholic	6	6	5	27	16
'Christian'	—	—	2	—	—
Other (Spiritualist, etc.)	1	6	3	—	2
Presbyterian, etc.	—	—	—	—	—

(b) 'Exploring English Character'

	South-East	South-West	Mid-lands	North-West	North-East
Jewish	1	—	—	—	—
Church of England	62	63	59	53	51
Church of Scotland	—	—	—	—	—
Baptist	3	3	4	2	2
Congregational	3	2	2	3	2
Methodist	6	9	12	9	18
Roman Catholic	7	3	7	14	7
'Christian'	3	4	3	2	2
Other (Spiritualist, etc.)	4	2	2	4	2
Presbyterian, etc.	5	9	7	5	9

Since the respondents in *Exploring English Character* were confined to England, the Church of Scotland was not included as such; but the group who described themselves as Presbyterian may have belonged to this sect, as may some who called themselves Nonconformists or Protestants. These exceptions apart, the distribution of denominations in the two samples is so similar as to enhance confidence in the representativeness of both of them.

Table XLIV

How often do You Normally attend a Church Service?
(Question 5c)

(Code for columns: A = More than once a week; B = Weekly; C = Less than once a week, but up to and including once a month; D = Less than once a month; E = Special occasions only; F = Never; G = No answer. * = less than .5%.)

(a) Present survey

	A	B	C	D	E	F	G
Total	2	15	13	16	35	17	2
Male	2	12	12	17	39	16	2
Female	3	18	14	14	31	18	2
Regions							
South-East	2	9	12	17	39	19	2
South-West	2	15	19	21	31	12	—
Midlands	—	13	14	21	34	18	—
North-West	—	26	5	14	33	22	—
North-East	4	15	15	5	39	15	—

(b) 'Exploring English Character'

	A	B	C	D	E	F	G
Total	6	9	8	11	59	7	—
Male	5	7	6	9	64	9	*
Female	7	11	11	13	52	5	*
Regions							
South-East	4	8	8	10	61	9	*
South-West	5	10	13	15	50	6	1
Midlands	7	9	8	10	60	6	—
North-West	8	9	8	12	58	4	1
North-East	7	10	8	10	59	6	*

The category of 'special occasions only' was represented in *Exploring English Character* by two alternatives: 'once or twice a year' and 'only for weddings and funerals'; and it seems likely that the greater number of respondents for 'never' in the present survey may be accounted for by the fact that quite a number of those interviewed did not count weddings or funerals as 'attending a church service'. If the two columns of 'special occasions' and 'never' are combined, a fairly consistent profile of the English majority for whom church-going plays a minimal role can be obtained. The greater proportion of people who attend church more than once a week in the respondents to *Exploring English Character* may be in part explained by the fact that there were a number of students, with compulsory church-going, in this survey and also more people from small country villages.

TABLE XLV

DO YOU EVER SAY ANY PRIVATE PRAYERS? HOW OFTEN?
(*Question 5d*)

(*Code for columns*: A = More than once a day; B = Daily; C = Less frequently; D = Special occasions only; E = Never; F = No answer.)

(*a*) *Present survey*

	A	B	C	D	E	F
Total	9	38	18	7	26	1
Male	3	23	22	7	43	1
Female	15	50	15	7	13	—
Regions						
South-East	8	33	18	7	26	2
South-West	10	36	21	8	23	2
Midlands	13	40	18	3	23	3
North-West	7	43	26	5	19	—
North-East	9	49	9	9	24	—

(*b*) *'Exploring English Character'*

	A	B	C	D	E	F
Total	11	33	28	16	14	1
Male	6	25	32	17	21	1
Female	16	42	24	14	5	2

Regions

South-East	10	33	27	17	16	1
South-West	11	36	30	15	11	1
Midlands	11	29	32	18	13	1
North-West	13	37	26	13	13	1
North-East	10	32	29	16	15	2

In *Exploring English Character* the categories representing 'less frequently' and 'special occasions only' were phrased as 'very seldom' and 'only in peril and grief'; since the informants in the present survey were all fairly recently bereaved the wording chosen was different, and this may account for the disparities between the two columns. If they are summated the differences become much less marked. The differences between the sexes and between the regions in the employment of private prayer seem consistent in the two samples.

TABLE XLVI

Do You BELIEVE IN THE DEVIL? (*Question 5e*)

	Present survey			'Exploring English Character'		
	Yes	No	Uncertain, No answer	Yes	No	Uncertain, No answer
Total	25	63	12	20	60	20
Male	22	72	6	17	67	16
Female	27	57	16	24	51	25
Regions						
South-East	21	66	13	19	62	19
South-West	17	58	25	23	58	22
Midlands	21	68	11	19	62	19
North-West	41	57	2	22	59	19
North-East	28	63	9	18	59	23

TABLE XLVII

Do You believe in an Afterlife? (*Question 5f*)

	Present survey			'Exploring English Character'		
	Yes	No	Uncertain, No answer	Yes	No	Uncertain, No answer
Total	49	25	26	47	22	31
Male	41	36	23	39	28	33
Female	55	16	29	56	14	30
Regions						
South-East	47	33	20	48	22	30
South-West	45	15	40	50	19	31
Midlands	50	24	26	43	24	33
North-West	37	36	27	48	21	31
North-East	60	20	20	44	22	34

The similarities in the totals, and the proportions of believers and sceptics among men and women in these two tables are very striking. One might have expected that a sample selected for recent bereavement would express a greater belief in an afterlife than would a group of volunteers; but this is not the case. On the basis of these close similarities, I consider that these tables do depict the contemporary patterns of belief and scepticism in England. I can only account for the apparent disparity in the case of one or two of the regional figures, especially in the North-West, by the difference in the proportion of Roman Catholics (Table XLII) in the two surveys.

TABLE XLVIII

IF YOU BELIEVE IN AN AFTERLIFE, WHAT WILL IT BE LIKE?
(*Question* 5g)

	Present survey N=174			'Exploring English Character' N=2325		
	Total	Male	Female	Total	Male	Female
Scriptural Heaven and Hell (reference to Judgment)	3	2	4	13	14	12
Scriptural Heaven (reference to God or Jesus)	4	3	5	9	11	7
Not like scriptural heaven	1	2	1	3	5	2
Beauty, rest, peace	8	4	11	15	12	19
Absence of evil, worry	4	3	4	11	10	12
Rejoining loved ones	9	2	14	9	6	11
Watching over loved ones	2	1	3	3	3	3
Like this life	5	5	5	11	12	11
Reincarnation	4	4	4	11	11	10
Life on another planet	1	1	—	2	1	2
No idea	15	17	13	20	19	20

(NOTE: Answers add up to more than 100 per cent since some respondents gave replies which fitted into more than one category.)

It is interesting to note that the bereaved gave even fewer dogmatically orthodox views on the afterlife than did the

volunteer sample; and also the relative popularity among bereaved women of the notions of rejoining one's loved ones
and of the non-religious concept of beauty, rest and peace.

I think the comparison of these two sets of tables demonstrates the fact that, although religious services are practically
universal at cremations and funerals, and although the only
currently accepted consolations for death are couched in religious terms, the experience of bereavement does not enhance the mourners' faith nor increase their public or private
practice of religion.

APPENDIX FOUR

THE PORNOGRAPHY OF DEATH

(NOTE: Since I have had occasion to refer to this essay more than
once in the preceding pages, and since it contains many of my earlier
ideas on the subject, I have thought it desirable to reprint it here, in
the interests of inclusivity. This article was first published in *En-
counter* in October, 1955; it was subsequently printed in several other
contexts in Great Britain and the United States and translated into
several European languages.)

> 'Birth, and copulation, and death.
> That's all the facts when you come to brass tacks;
> Birth, and copulation, and death.'
>   T. S. Eliot, *Sweeney Agonistes* (1932)

Pornography is, no doubt, the opposite face, the shadow, of
prudery, whereas obscenity is an aspect of seemliness. No
society has been recorded which has not its rules of seemliness, of words or actions which arouse discomfort and embarrassment in some contexts, though they are essential in
others. The people before whom one must maintain a watch-
ful seemliness vary from society to society: all people of the
opposite sex, or all juniors, or all elders, or one's parents-in-

law, or one's social superiors or inferiors, or one's grandchildren have been selected in different societies as groups in whose presence the employment of certain words or the performance of certain actions would be considered offensive; and then these words or actions become charged with affect. There is a tendency for these words and actions to be related to sex and excretion, but this is neither necessary nor universal; according to Malinowski, the Trobrianders surround eating with as much shame as excretion; and in other societies personal names or aspects of ritual come under the same taboos.

Rules of seemliness are apparently universal; and the non-observance of these rules, or anecdotes which involve the breaking of the rules, provoke that peculiar type of laughter which seems identical the world over; however little one may know about a strange society, however little one may know about the functions of laughter in that society (and these can be very various) one can immediately tell when people are laughing at an obscene joke. The topper of the joke may be 'And then he ate the whole meal in front of them!', or 'She used her husband's name in the presence of his mother!', but the laughter is the same; the taboos of seemliness have been broken and the result is hilarious. Typically, such laughter is confined to one-sex groups and is more general with the young, just entering into the complexities of adult life.

Obscenity then is a universal, an aspect of man and woman living in society; everywhere and at all times there are words and actions which, when misplaced, can produce shock, social embarrassment and laughter. Pornography on the other hand, the description of tabooed activities to produce hallucination or delusion, seems to be a very much rarer phenomenon. It probably can only arise in literate societies, and we certainly have no records of it for non-literate ones; for whereas the enjoyment of obscenity is predominantly social, the enjoyment of pornography is predominantly private. The fantasies from which pornography derives could of course be generated in any society; but it seems doubtful whether they would ever be communicated without the intermediary of literacy.

The one possible exception to this generalization is the use of plastic arts without any letterpress. I have never felt quite certain that the three-dimensional *poses plastiques* on so many Hindu temples (notably the 'Black Pagoda' at Konarak) have really the highfalutin Worship of the Life Force or Glorification of the Creative Aspect of Sex which their apologists claim for them; many of them seem to me very like 'feelthy' pictures, despite the skill with which they are executed. There are too the erotic woodcuts of Japan; but quite a lot of evidence suggests that these are thought of as laughter-provoking (i.e. obscene) by the Japanese themselves. We have no knowledge of the functions of the Peruvian pottery.

As far as my knowledge goes, the only Asian society which had a long-standing tradition of pornographic literature is China; and, it would appear, social life under the Manchus was surrounded by much the same haze of prudery as distinguished the nineteenth century in much of Europe and the Americas, even though the emphasis fell rather differently; women's deformed feet seem to have been the greatest focus of peeking and sniggering, rather than their ankles or the cleft between their breasts; but by and large life in Manchu China seems to have been nearly as full of 'unmentionables' as life in Victoria's heyday.

Pornography would appear to be a concomitant of prudery, and usually the periods of the greatest production of pornography have also been the periods of the most rampant prudery. In contrast to obscenity, which is chiefly defined by situation, prudery is defined by subject; some aspect of human experience is treated as inherently shameful or abhorrent, so that it can never be discussed or referred to openly, and experience of it tends to be clandestine and accompanied by feelings of guilt and unworthiness. The unmentionable aspect of experience then tends to become a subject for much private fantasy, more or less realistic, fantasy charged with pleasurable guilt or guilty pleasure; and those whose power of fantasy is weak, or whose demand is insatiable, constitute a market for the printed fantasies of the pornographer.

Traditionally, and in the lexicographic meaning of the term, pornography has been concerned with sexuality. For the greater part of the last two hundred years copulation and (at least in the mid-Victorian decades) birth were the 'unmentionables' of the triad of basic human experiences which 'are all the facts when you come to brass tacks', around which so much private fantasy and semi-clandestine pornography were erected. During most of this period death was no mystery, except in the sense that death is always a mystery. Children were encouraged to think about death, their own deaths and the edifying or cautionary death-beds of others. It can have been a rare individual who, in the 19th century with its high mortality, had not witnessed at least one actual dying, as well as paying their respect to 'beautiful corpses'; funerals were the occasion of the greatest display for working class, middle class, and aristocrat. The cemetery was the centre of every old-established village, and they were prominent in most towns. It was fairly late in the 19th century when the execution of criminals ceased to be a public holiday as well as a public warning. Mr. Fairchild had no difficulty in finding a suitably garnished gibbet for his moral lesson.

In the 20th century, however, there seems to have been an unremarked shift in prudery; whereas copulation has become more and more 'mentionable', particularly in the Anglo-Saxon societies, death has become more and more 'unmentionable' *as a natural process*. I cannot recollect a novel or play of the last twenty years or so which has a 'death-bed scene' in it, describing in any detail the death 'from natural causes' of a major character; this topic was a set piece for most of the eminent Victorian and Edwardian writers, evoking their finest prose and their most elaborate technical effects to produce the greatest amount of pathos or edification.

One of the reasons, I imagine, for this plethora of death-bed scenes—apart from their intrinsic emotional and religious content—was that it was one of the relatively few experiences that an author could be fairly sure would have been shared by the vast majority of his readers. Questioning my old acquaintances, I cannot find one over the age of sixty who did not witness the agony of at least one near relative; I do not think I know a single person under the age of thirty who has had a similar experience. Of course my acquaintance is neither very extensive nor particularly representative; but in this instance I do think it is typical of the change of attitude and 'exposure'.

The natural processes of corruption and decay have become disgusting, as disgusting as the natural processes of birth and copulation were a century ago; preoccupation about such processes is (or was) morbid and unhealthy, to be discouraged in all and punished in the young. Our great-grandparents were told that babies were found under gooseberry bushes or cabbages; our children are likely to be told that those who have passed on (fie! on the gross Anglo-Saxon monosyllable) are changed into flowers, or lie at rest in lovely gardens. The ugly facts are relentlessly hidden; the art of the embalmers is an art of complete denial.

It seems possible to trace a connection between the shift of taboos and the shift in religious beliefs. In the 19th century most of the inhabitants of Protestant countries seem to have subscribed to the Pauline beliefs in the sinfulness of the body and the certainty of the afterlife. 'So also is the resurrection of the dead. It is sown in corruption; it is raised in incorruption: it is sown in dishonour; it is raised in glory.' It was possible to insist on the corruption of the dead body, and the dishonour of its begetting, while there was a living belief in the incorruption and the glory of the immortal part. But in England, at any rate, belief in the future life as taught in Christian doctrine is very uncommon today even in the minority who make church-going or prayer a consistent part of their lives; and without some such belief natural death and physical decomposition have become too horrible to contemplate or to discuss. It seems symptomatic that the contemporary sect of Christian Science should deny the fact of physical death, even to the extent (so it is said) of refusing to allow the word to be printed in the *Christian Science Monitor*.

During the last half-century public health measures and improved preventive medicine have made natural death among the younger members of the population much more uncommon than it had been in earlier periods, so that a death in the family, save in the fullness of time, became a relatively uncommon incident in home life; and, simultaneously, violent death increased in a manner unparalleled in human history. Wars and revolutions, concentration camps and gang feuds were the most publicized of the causes for these violent deaths; but the diffusion of the automobile, with its constant and unnoticed toll of fatal accidents, may well have been most influential in bringing the possibility of violent death into the expectations of law-abiding people in time of peace. While natural death became more and more smothered in prudery, violent death has played an ever-growing part in the fantasies offered to mass audiences—detective stories, thrillers, Westerns, war stories, spy stories, science fiction, and eventually horror comics.

There seem to be a number of parallels between the fantasies which titillate our curiosity about the mystery of sex, and those which titillate our curiosity about the mystery of death. In both types of fantasy, the emotions which are typically concomitant of the acts—love or grief—are paid little or no attention, while the sensations are enhanced as much as a customary poverty of language permits. If marital intercourse be considered the natural expression of sex for most of humanity most of the time, then 'natural sex' plays as little role as 'natural death' (the ham-fisted attempts of D. H. Lawrence and Jules Romains to describe 'natural sex' realistically but high-mindedly prove the rule). Neither type of fantasy can have any real development, for once the protagonist has done something, he or she must proceed to do something else, with or to somebody else, more refined, more complicated, or more sensational than what had occurred before. This somebody else is not a person; it is either a set of genitals, with or without secondary sexual characteristics, or a body, perhaps capable of suffering pain as well as death. Since most languages are relatively poor in words or constructions to express intense pleasure or intense pain, the written portions of both types of fantasy abound in onomatopoeic conglomerations of letters meant to evoke the sighs, gasps, groans, screams, and rattles concomitant to the described actions. Both types of fantasy rely heavily on adjective and simile. Both types of fantasy are completely unrealistic, since they ignore all physical, social, or legal limitations, and both types have complete hallucination of the reader or viewer as their object.

There seems little question that the instinct of those censorious busybodies preoccupied with other people's morals was correct when they linked the pornography of death with the pornography of sex. This, however, seems to be the only thing which has been correct in their deductions or attempted actions. There is no valid evidence to suggest that either type of pornography is an incitement to action; rather are they substitute gratifications. The belief that such hallucinatory works would incite their readers to copy the actions depicted would seem to be indirect homage to the late Oscar Wilde, who described such a process in *The Portrait of Dorian Gray*; I know of no authenticated parallels in real life, though investigators and magistrates with bees in their bonnets can usually persuade juvenile delinquents to admit to exposure to whatever medium of mass communication they are choosing to make a scapegoat.

Despite some gifted precursors, such as Andréa de Nerciat or Edgar Allan Poe, most works in both pornographies are aesthetically objectionable; but it is questionable whether, from the purely aesthetic point of view, there is much more to be said for the greater part of the more anodyne fare provided by contemporary mass media of communication. Psy-

chological Utopians tend to condemn substitute gratifications
as such, at least where copulation is involved; they have so
far been chary in dealing with death.

Nevertheless, people have to come to terms with the basic
facts of birth, copulation and death, and somehow accept
their implications; if social prudery prevents this being done
in an open and dignified fashion, then it will be done sur-
reptitiously. If we dislike the modern pornography of death,
then we must give back to death—natural death—its parade
and publicity, readmit grief and mourning. If we make death
unmentionable in polite society—'not before the children'—we
almost ensure the continuation of the 'horror comic'. No cen-
sorship has ever been really effective.

BIBLIOGRAPHY

(1) BOWLBY, J. (1960) 'Grief and Mourning in Infancy and Early Childhood', in *The Psychoanalytic Study of the Child*, Vol. XV.

(2) BOWLBY, J. (1961) 'Processes of Mourning', *International Journal of Psycho-Analysis*, Vol. XLII, parts 4–5.

(3) DEVEREUX, G. (1961) *Mohave Ethnopsychiatry and Suicide*, (Bureau of American Ethnology).

(4) ELIOT, T. D. (1954) 'Bereavement: Inevitable but not Insurmountable', in *Family, Marriage and Parenthood* edited by Becker and Hill (Boston: Heath, 1955).

(5) ENGEL, G. (1961) 'Is Grief a Disease?' *Psychosomatic Medicine*, Vol. 23.

(6) FEIFEL, H. (1959) 'Attitudes Toward Death in Some Normal and Mentally Ill Populations' in *The Meaning of Death* edited by H. Feifel (New York: McGraw-Hill Book Co. 1959).

(7) FREUD, S. 'Mourning and Melancholia' in *The Complete Psychological Works of Sigmund Freud*, Standard Edition, Vol. 14, pp. 237–258 (New York: Macmillan).

(8) GORER, G. (1962) *Africa Dances* (New York: Norton).

(9) GORER, G. *Exploring English Character* (Criterion).

(10) HARMER, R. M. (1963) *The High Cost of Dying* (New York: Cromwell-Collier Press).

(11) JONES, E. (1953, 1955) *Sigmund Freud: Life and Work* (London: Hogarth Press).

(12) KASPER, A. M. (1959) 'The Doctor and Death', in *The Meaning of Death*, ed. Feifel.

(13) KLEIN, M. (1940) 'Mourning and Its Relation to

Manic-Depressive States', in *Contributions to Psycho-Analysis 1921–1945* (New York: Hillary).

(14) LEHRMAN, S. R. (1956) 'Reactions to Untimely Death', *Psychiatry Quarterly*, Vol. XXX.

(15) LINDEMANN, E. (1944) 'Symptomatology and Management of Acute Grief', *American Journal of Psychiatry*, Vol. CI.

(16) MANDELBAUM, D. G. (1959) 'Social Uses of Funeral Rites', in *The Meaning of Death*, ed. Feifel.

(17) MARRIS, P. (1958) *Widows and Their Families* (London: Routledge).

(18) MITFORD, J. (1963) *The American Way of Death* (New York: Simon & Schuster).

(19) POLSON, C. J. (1962) (editor) *The Disposal of the Dead* (London: English Universities Press).

(20) TITMUSS, R. (1958) *Essays on 'The Welfare State'* (London: Allen and Unwin).

(21) WAUGH, E. (1948) *The Loved One* (New York: Little).

(22) WYNN, M. (1964) *Fatherless Families* (London: Joseph).

(23) ZBOROWSKI, M. and HERZOG, E. (1952) *Life is with People* (New York: International Universities Press).

INDEX OF INFORMANTS QUOTED
MORE THAN ONCE

18. 55-year-old wife of a professional man in the Midlands. Nominal C. of E. Lost brother. 16, 31

19. 70-year-old widow of a worker in gas board in Scotland. C. of E. Lost husband. 26, 38, 56, 81

20. 48-year-old clerical assistant (male) in the North-East. C. of E. Lost mother. 27, 48

21. 45-year-old widow of a shopkeeper in the North-West. Congregationalist. Lost husband. 28, 38, 52, 73, 104

22. 85-year-old widow of a professional service officer in the South-West. C. of E. Lost husband. 28, 35, 56, 106, 111

23. 40-ish widow of a coal-merchant and 19-year-old daughter in Scotland. Nominal Church of Scotland. Lost husband. (vdl. father). 29, 105, 110

24. 60-year-old married proprietor of a small shop in Scotland. Church of Scotland. Lost mother. 31, 34, 45, 88, 101

25. 48-year-old butcher in Scotland. Church of Scotland. Widowed and remarried. 32, 112, 116

26. 45-year-old wife of a disabled soldier in the South-West. Student of Yoga. Lost brother and sister. 32, 44, 67, 118

27. 73-year-old widowed old-age pensioner in the North-East. Christian Scientist. Lost a sister. 32, 66

28. 63-year-old widower running own small business in the South-West. Spiritualist. Lost brother. 32, 65

29. 53-year-old widow of a baker in Scotland. Church of Scotland. Lost husband. 34, 44, 52, 84, 103, 111, 125

30. 71-year-old old-age pensioner, former factory worker, in Scotland. Nominal Church of Scotland. Lost wife. 34, 115

31. 67-year-old widow of a senior civil servant in the South-West. Methodist. Lost husband. 34, 46, 72, 87, 102, 108

32. 64-year-old widow of a regular serviceman (retired) in the South-West. Nominal C. of E. Lost husband. 35, 56, 70, 108, 111, 148

33. 50-ish widow of a businessman in the Midlands. C. of E. Lost husband. 36, 59, 109, 111

34. 67-year-old widow of a colliery maintenance engineer in the North-East. C. of E. Lost husband. 36, 42, 62, 86, 106, 111

35. 74-year-old widow in the North-West. Old-age pensioner. C. of E. Lost a brother. 36, 43, 56, 109

36. 48-year-old widow of a self-employed taxi-driver in the North-East. Nominal C. of E. Lost husband. 38, 45, 50, 58, 62, 86, 109, 111

37. 71-year-old wife of a pensioned bricklayer in the South-East. C. of E. Lost youngest sister. 44, 53, 85, 98, 120

38. 59-year-old fitter in the North-East. C. of E. Lost father and mother. 44, 68, 117

39. 51-year-old unmarried employee in local government in Scotland. C. of E. Lost mother. 45, 97

40. 17-year-old storeman in the Midlands. Nominal C. of E. Lost father. 45, 59, 84, 96

41. 58-year-old cement worker in the South-East. Nominal C. of E. Lost wife. 45, 86, 97, 113

42. 55-year-old local government official in the South-East. Nominal C. of E. Lost wife. 52, 83, 86, 112

43. 54-year-old van-driver in the South-West. No denomination. Lost elder sister. 54, 84, 119

44. 61-year-old widow of a businessman in the Midlands. C. of E. Lost husband and adult spastic son. 55, 83, 106, 109, 111, 125

45. 42-year-old wife of local government official in South-East. C. of E. Lost mother. 55, 69

46. 54-year-old widow of a process-worker in the South-East. Nominal C. of E. Lost husband. 55, 89, 111

47. 48-year-old shopkeeper in the South-East. Nominal C. of E. Lost wife. 57, 61, 84, 112, 115

48. 23-year-old betrothed manageress of a shop in the Midlands. Nominal C. of E. Lost father. 59, 95

49. 70-year-old old-age pensioner and wife in the North-West. Roman Catholic. Lost adult son. 59, 84, 123

50. 47-year-old married woman, full-time factory worker, in Scotland. Nominal Church of Scotland. Lost father. 61, 81, 94

51. 49-year-old widow working as bus conductress in the North-East. Nominal C. of E. Lost husband. 61, 71, 104, 111

52. 32-year-old caretaker of a block of flats in the North-East. Nominal C. of E. Lost father. 61, 82, 92

53. 44-year-old professional man in the South-West. No denomination. Lost 15-year-old son. 61, 123

54. 49-year-old widow, school caretaker in the South-East. Nominal C. of E. Lost elder sister. 68, 119

55. 57-year-old railway worker in the North-West. Nominal C. of E. Lost a brother. 68, 119, 126

56. 68-year-old widower in the South-East, old-age pensioner. Anti-religious. Lost three brothers. 68, 119

57. 41-year-old remarried wife of a school-teacher in the North-East. Nominal C. of E. Lost father and mother. 69, 111

58. 66-year-old retired tracer in the North-East. Nominal C. of E. Lost wife. 71, 89, 115

59. 41-year-old manager of a caravan site in the South-East. No denomination. Lost mother. 72, 97

60. 60-year-old widow of a senior civil servant in the South-West. C. of E. Lost husband. 72, 102

61. 20-ish daughter of an Australian businessman in the South-East. Presbyterian. Lost mother. 74, 97

62. 49-year-old widow of a professional man, working as a clerkess, in Scotland. Nominal Church of Scotland. Lost husband. 74, 96, 102, 103, 112

63. 55-year-old widowed and remarried businessman in the North-East. Jewish. Lost wife. 79, 112, 116

64. 50-ish widow of a skilled workman in Scotland. C. of E. Lost husband. 84, 96

65. 61-year-old manufacturer in the North-West. Methodist. Lost wife. 86, 89, 113

66. 66-year-old widower, old-age pensioner in the North-East. Roman Catholic. Lost adult son. 88, 122

67. 42-year-old miner in the Midlands. C. of E. Lost father. 92, 117

68. 79-year-old old-age pensioner in the South-East. Nominal C. of E. Lost husband. 106, 111

NOTE: *Informants 9, 10, 12, 13, 16, 17, 18, 20 were not interviewed by me. The quotations come from their answers to the questionnaire interviewers.*

THE LITERATURE OF
DEATH AND DYING

Abrahamsson, Hans. **The Origin of Death:** Studies in African Mythology. 1951

Alden, Timothy. **A Collection of American Epitaphs and Inscriptions with Occasional Notes.** Five vols. in two. 1814

Austin, Mary. **Experiences Facing Death.** 1931

Bacon, Francis. **The Historie of Life and Death with Observations Naturall and Experimentall for the Prolongation of Life.** 1638

Barth, Karl. **The Resurrection of the Dead.** 1933

Bataille, Georges. **Death and Sensuality:** A Study of Eroticism and the Taboo. 1962

Bichat, [Marie François] Xavier. **Physiological Researches on Life and Death.** 1827

Browne, Thomas. **Hydriotaphia.** 1927

Carrington, Hereward. **Death:** Its Causes and Phenomena with Special Reference to Immortality. 1921

Comper, Frances M. M., editor. **The Book of the Craft of Dying and Other Early English Tracts Concerning Death.** 1917

Death and the Visual Arts. 1976

Death as a Speculative Theme in Religious, Scientific, and Social Thought. 1976

Donne, John. **Biathanatos.** 1930

Farber, Maurice L. **Theory of Suicide.** 1968

Fechner, Gustav Theodor. **The Little Book of Life After Death.** 1904

Frazer, James George. **The Fear of the Dead in Primitive Religion.** Three vols. in one. 1933/1934/1936

Fulton, Robert. **A Bibliography on Death, Grief and Bereavement:** 1845-1975. 1976

Gorer, Geoffrey. **Death, Grief, and Mourning.** 1965

Gruman, Gerald J. **A History of Ideas About the Prolongation of Life.** 1966

Henry, Andrew F. and James F. Short, Jr. **Suicide and Homicide.** 1954

Howells, W[illiam] D[ean], et al. **In After Days;** Thoughts on the Future Life. 1910

Irion, Paul E. **The Funeral:** Vestige or Value? 1966

Landsberg, Paul-Louis. **The Experience of Death:** The Moral Problem of Suicide. 1953

Maeterlinck, Maurice. **Before the Great Silence.** 1937

Maeterlinck, Maurice. **Death.** 1912

Metchnikoff, Élie. **The Nature of Man:** Studies in Optimistic Philosophy. 1910

Metchnikoff, Élie. **The Prolongation of Life:** Optimistic Studies. 1908

Munk, William. **Euthanasia.** 1887

Osler, William. **Science and Immortality.** 1904

Return to Life: Two Imaginings of the Lazarus Theme. 1976

Stephens, C[harles] A[sbury]. **Natural Salvation:** The Message of Science. 1905

Sulzberger, Cyrus. **My Brother Death.** 1961

Taylor, Jeremy. **The Rule and Exercises of Holy Dying.** 1819

Walker, G[eorge] A[lfred]. **Gatherings from Graveyards.** 1839

Warthin, Aldred Scott. **The Physician of the Dance of Death.** 1931

Whiter, Walter. **Dissertation on the Disorder of Death.** 1819

Whyte, Florence. **The Dance of Death in Spain and Catalonia.** 1931

Wolfenstein, Martha. **Disaster:** A Psychological Essay. 1957

Worcester, Alfred. **The Care of the Aged, the Dying, and the Dead.** 1950

Zandee, J[an]. **Death as an Enemy According to Ancient Egyptian Conceptions.** 1960